THE BOOK OF DAMNATION

The Second Death

MARIE SMITH

The wages of sin is death, but the gift of God is eternal life.
(Romans 6: 23)

ARPress
45 Dan Road Suite 5
Canton MA 02021
Hotline: 1(888) 821-0229
Fax: 1(508) 545-7580

Ordering Information:
Quantity sales. Special discounts are available on quantity purchases by corporations, associations, and others. For details, contact the publisher at the address above.

Printed in the United States of America.

ISBN-13:   Paperback   979-8-89389-304-5
           eBook   979-8-89389-305-2

Library of Congress Control Number: 2024915209

To The Glory of God

Table of Contents

THE BOOK OF REVELATION

We are in the last days at a time when violence, murder, homosexuality, sexual immorality, human trafficking, sodomite, and false teaching. When evil and uncertainty is very much in our sight and growing daily. The world is looking for answers and some Christians are looking for encouragement to know who God is and strengthen their faith in the Lord. Many Christians and unsaved humanity don't know about the book of Revelation, and it purpose in the greater schemes of things that is happening. In my book, I draw upon years of biblical study and research to shed some light on a subject that is close and dear to the Lord heart for souls. We can see in the Book of Revelation many warnings throughout the book; there are many movies about the history and stories of the Seven Churches. What about the warnings and danger of the sins and no repentance of humanity in these churches and where their final destination will be. *The Book of Life* is for the saved and *The Book of Damnation* is for the unsaved.

There is no longer A Fear of God!

And do not fear those who kill the body but cannot kill the soul. But rather fear him (Jesus) who can destroy both soul and body in hell. (Matthew 10: 28).

The road to Hell is paved with the bones of priests and monks, and the skulls of Bishops are the lamp posts that light the path.

The road to hell is paved with the skulls of erring priests, with bishops as their signposts. (St. John Chrysostom, extract from St. John Chrysostom, Homily III on Acts 1:12)

WARNING

My book: **The Angels of the Seven Churches:** is a <u>**Warning**</u> to Humanity, and All Nations, World Leaders, State, City, County, All Civil Officials, Shepherds and Five-Fold Ministries, and Churches.

The Lord gave me a **Vision of Hell:**

I had a vision where the angel of the Lord took me to heaven and Jesus. Jesus took my hand and spoke, do not let go of my hand no matter what you see. Then he waved his hand, the veil lifted, we went down the steps, and I saw a giant demon and many people rows after rows; you could not count. I asked the Lord who is all these people, and Jesus answered, "these are my shepherds that have led my flock astray", I asked him if any of the shepherds made it into heaven because it looked like trillions of shepherds in hell. He did not answer. Jesus waves his hand and uncovers some shepherd's faces; some I knew, some I did not realize until later.

Then he showed a mighty teacher in the word of God I knew in a caged crying; she said, "I thought they were teaching me right". Then Jesus said, did you ask me if they are teaching you right; she said "No" and started to cry; He said, "Judgment has been set!" I did not feel the heat in hell nor hear their screams or torture of the people.

Then Jesus told me to write this book: The Angels of The Seven Churches. The world leaders, shepherds, and the churches are asleep and need to wake up! Then fix themselves and take to the Lord in Prayer.

1. **The World leaders, State, County, and City Officials, Shepherds, and Churches:**

Isaiah 9:16 For the leaders of these peoples cause them to err, and those they lead are destroyed.

2. **Christian Witches:**

1 Samuel 15: 23 For rebellion is the sin of witchcraft, and stubbornness is iniquity and idolatry. Because you have rejected the Word of the Lord, He also has rejected you from being king.

3. **Irresponsible Shepherds:** Ezekiel 34:1-10,

Ezekiel Chapter 34:1-10

Ezekiel 34:1 "And the word of the LORD came unto me, saying,"

It is against a brand-new prophecy. Ezekiel turns from the people to their leaders, who have the most significant guilt.

From this chapter on, Ezekiel's messages are primarily comforting, telling of God's grace and faithfulness to His covenant promises.

Ezekiel 34:2 "Son of man, prophesy against the shepherds of Israel, prophesy, and say unto them, thus saith the Lord GOD unto the shepherds; Woe be to the shepherds of Israel that do feed themselves! Should not the shepherds feed the flocks?"

"Prophesy against the shepherds of Israel": The reference was to pre-exilic leaders such as kings, priests, and prophets - their civil leaders, as well as their spiritual leaders, which means those false ones who fleeced the flock for personal gain (verses 3-4), rather than fed or led righteously. It stands in contrast to the Lord as Shepherd.

These Scriptures also have a meaning for the Jews and Christians. We will try to look at both as we go along. These verses' beginning is a reprimand for not caring for the sheep. The kings and preachers must now be careful in feeding the sheep. That is the primary job of a shepherd.

Ezekiel 34:3 "Ye eat the fat, and ye clothe you with the wool, ye kill them that are fed, but ye feed not the flock."

It speaks of those who take from the sheep and give nothing. We see in some churches today that ministers are living far above the conditions of their people and are not teaching them true doctrine or the dangers of not living according to God's Holy Word.

Ezekiel 34:4 "The diseased have ye not strengthened, neither have ye healed that which was sick, neither have ye bound up [that which was] broken, neither have ye brought again that which were driven away, neither have ye sought that which was lost; but with force and with cruelty have ye ruled them."

Some treat the church as a hotel for saints and not a hospital for sinners.

Mark 2:17 "When Jesus heard it, he saith unto them, They that are whole have no need of the physician, but they that are sick: I came not to call the righteous, but sinners to repentance."

Those whose spirits are sick need us. The weak sheep need more care than the healthy ones. A good shepherd keeps his sheep together with love, patience, and kindness, not by driving them. Jesus told the parable about the Shepherd that left the 99 and went to find the one that lost. The 23rd Psalm describes the good Shepherd.

Ezekiel 34:5 "And they were scattered because there is no shepherd: and they became meat to all the beasts of the field when they were scattered."

When the flock is divided, it is easy prey for the wolves. They get one sheep off from the others and kill him. It is true of the church. Together we stand; divided, we fall. The wolf is not afraid of the sheep but scared of the Shepherd. The Shepherd drives the wolf away and saves the sheep.

In verse above, there is no shepherd. The sheep are easy prey. Therefore, a Christian needs fellowship in a church with other Christians and to be under the care of a pastor. There is safety in the numbers, and the pastor protects the single member. The pastor is a protector and guide.

The beasts of the field pictured here picture the nations that prey on Israel (Dan. 7:3-7), though it could include actual wild beasts (as in 14:21, 34:25, and 28).

Ezekiel 34:6 "My sheep wandered through all the mountains, and upon every high hill: yea, my flock was scattered upon all the face of the earth, and none did search or seek after them."

Holding a civil office or an office in a church carries a grave responsibility. We should not take office if we have not weighed the cost and are willing to sacrifice to do a good job. The loss of the world today is like those sheep in the mountains. We must go and get them.

To be saved yourself is excellent, but God called His workers to seek out the lost. How can they be saved without hearing? They must listen to the Word of God to be saved.

Ezekiel 34:7 "Therefore, ye shepherds, hear the word of the LORD."

It is not just an idle statement but a warning to the ministers of today and the leaders of the Jews then.

Ezekiel 34:8 "As I live, saith the Lord GOD, surely because my flock became a prey, and my flock became meat to every beast of the field because there was no shepherd, neither did my shepherds search for my flock, but the shepherds fed themselves, and fed not my flock;"

All who work in the ministry should be ministering because God called them to that task, not as a way of making a living. Of course, you must have a living, but it should not be your reason for accepting a specific job.

The food that the minister of God must bring the flock is the pure Word of God. The Word cannot be watered down, or it will not nourish the sheep.

The sheep will not be in danger of straying away when they are well-fed. When they know the Word of God, they are not as quickly drawn away to false prophets.

Ezekiel 34:9 "Therefore, O ye shepherds, hear the word of the LORD;"

It is no idle threat, as proven by the case of King Zedekiah (Jer. 52:10-11).

Ezekiel 34:10 "Thus saith the Lord GOD; Behold, I am against the shepherds; and I will require my flock at their hand and cause them to cease from feeding the flock; neither shall the shepherds feed themselves anymore; for I will deliver my flock from their mouth, that they may not be meat for them."

God will not allow a leader to go on who does not care for the people. These shepherds, who do not care for the sheep, will be replaced by someone who cares for the sheep. The owner (God) does not want to lose his sheep. The critical Word in the verse above is a mouth full. He will deliver them from his mouth.

Angels of the Seven Churches

The mystery of the seven stars you saw in my right hand and the seven golden lampstands.

The Seven Stars: are the angels of the seven churches, and

The Seven Lampstands: which you saw, are the seven churches (Rev. 1:20).

Revelation 2:

To the angel of the church of Ephesus, write, The Loveless Church:

Nevertheless, I have this against you, that you have left your first love. Remember, therefore, from where you have fallen, repent and do the first works, or else I will come to you quickly and remove your lampstand from its place -unless you repent. To him who overcomes, I will give to eat from the Tree of Life, which is amid the paradise of God.

Let him hear what the Spirit says to the churches who have an ear. (Holy Bible, KJV, 2012).

To the angel of the church in Smyrna writes, The Persecuted Church:

I know the blasphemy of those who say they are Jews and are not but are a synagogue of Satan. Do not fear any of those things which you are about to suffer. Indeed, the devil is about to throw some of you into prison, that you may be tested, and you will have tribulation for ten days. Be faithful until death, and I will give the crown of life. The second death shall not hurt him who overcomes.

Let him hear what the Spirit says to the churches who have an ear. (Holy Bible, KJV, 2012).

To the church's angel in Pergamos write, The Compromising Church:

I know your works, where you dwell, where Satan's throne is. But I have a few things against you because you have; they're those who hold the doctrine of Balaam, who taught Balak to put a stumbling block before the children of Israel, to eat things sacrificed to idols, and commit sexual immorality. Repent, or else I will come to you quickly and fight against them with the sword of my mouth. Let him hear what the Spirit says to the churches who have an ear. To him who overcomes, I will give him a Whitestone and a new name written on the stone that no one knows except him who receives it.

Let him hear what the Spirit says to the churches who have an ear. (Holy Bible, KJV, 2012).

To the church's angel in Thyatira, write The Corrupt Church:

Nevertheless, I have a few things against you because you allow that woman Jezebel, who calls herself prophetess, to teach and seduce my servants to commit sexual immorality and eat things sacrificed to idols. And I gave her time to repent of her sexual sin, and she did not repent. I will cast her into a sickbed and those who commit adultery with her into great tribulation unless they repent of their deed.

Let him hear what the Spirit says to the churches who have an ear. (Holy Bible, KJV, 2012).

Revelation 3:

To the angel of the church in Sardis, write The Dead Church:

Remember therefore how you have received and heard; hold fast and repent, therefore, if you do not watch, I will come upon you as a thief, and you will not know what hour I will come upon you. You have a few names even in Sardis who have not defiled their garments, and they shall walk with Me in white, for they are worthy. He who comes shall be clothed in white garments, and I will not blot out his name from the Book of Life, but I will confess his name before My Father and before His angels.

Let him hear what the Spirit says to the churches who have an ear. (Holy Bible, KJV, 2012).

To the church's angel in Philadelphia, write, The Faithful Church:

Behold, I am coming quickly! Hold fast what you have, that no one may take your crown. He who overcomes, I will make him a pillar in the temple of My God, and he shall go out no more. I will write on him the name of My God and the name of the city of My God, the New Jerusalem, which comes down out of heaven from My God. And I will Write Him My new name.

Let him hear what the Spirit says to the churches who have an ear. (Holy Bible, KJV, 2012).

To the angel of the church of the Laodiceans write, The Lukewarm Church:

Because you say, I am rich, have become wealthy, and need nothing- and do not know that you are wretched, miserable, poor, blind and naked- I counsel you to buy from Me gold refined in the fire, that you may be rich; and white garments, that you may be clothed, that the shame of your nakedness may not be revealed; and anoint your eyes with eye salve, that you may see. As many as I love, I rebuke and chasten. Behold, I stand at the door and knock. If anyone hears My voice and opens the door, I will come into him and dine with him, and he with Me. I will grant to sit with Me on My Throne to him who overcomes, as I also overcame and sat down with My Father on His throne.

Let him hear what the Spirit says to the churches who have an ear. (Holy Bible, KJV, 2012).

References:

KJV, The Holy Bible, (2012). (ALL RIGHTS RESERVED). The Holy Bible KJV. Knoxville, TN 37921: Power Publishing Corporation.

NKJV, The Holy Bible, (2012). Spiritual Warfare Bible. Lake Mary, Florida 32746: Charisma House.

Unknown. (12th Century). Old and New Testaments. Rome: Canonical Books

INTRODUCTION

The people who are not saved will suffer everlasting torment in the lake of fire. These four articles in this series:

- The case for destruction.

- The smoke of their torment goes up forever (Rev 14:9-11)

- The lake of fire is the second death. (Rev 20:10)

- The proof of eternal torment

The case for destruction

After God created man (Gen 2:7), God told Adam that he would die if he ate from the tree of knowledge of good and evil (Gen 2:17). Man, therefore, after he was created, was not an immortal being.

After man sinned, God drove him out of the garden to prevent him from eating from the Tree of Life "and live forever" (Gen 3:22). In the circumstance of the creation explanation, this was a spiritual death sentence. Unless something changed, man's death would be his final- end. But something did change:" God so loved the world, that He gave His only begotten Son, that whoever believes in Him shall not perish but have eternal life" (John 3:16).

- Those who do not believe in Jesus Christ will "perish."

- Whoever believes in Him shall have "eternal life."

- Non-believers will perish.

The opposite of eternal life is death.

In many of the examples above, the fate of the lost is explained as "death." That is not the first and temporary death that all people face. Instead, it is that dreadful and permanent death that only sinners will suffer, which Revelation refers to as *"the second death"* (Rev 20:14; cf. 20:6; 21:8). "He who believes Him who sent me, has eternal life, and has passed out of death into life" (John 5:24).

"The wages of sin is death, but the free gift of God is eternal life" (Rom 6:23).

Our Savior Jesus will get rid of death and bring life and immortality to light" (2 Tim 1:10). For other such statements, (Romans 6:16, 21-22; 8:13; 5:21 or Galatians 6:8).

These sections between "death" and "eternal life" utterly contradict the distinction between eternal life in happiness and eternal life in torment that the established principle describes.

The smoke of their torment will rise forever (Rev 14:9-11).

In the series on Death, Eternal Life, and Eternal Torment. People with the mark of the beast will be tormented in fire and brimstone, and the smoke of their torment will go up forever (Rev 14:9-11). For example, they will be crushed in Christ's presence, and they will remain forever in hell. Revelation does not use the word "hell." Still, the third angel (Rev 14:9) warns the people of the world (Rev 14:6) that a person who accepts the mark of the beast himself will drink the wine of the wrath of God, which is mixed in full power in the cup of his anger. He will be tormented with fire and brimstone in the presence of the holy angels and the Lamb. And the smoke of their torment goes up forever and ever; they have no rest day and night. (Rev 14:10-11). Paul's constant vision that sinners will die (Rom 6:23), and with Christ's warning that God "can destroy both soul and body in hell" (Matt 10:28)?

The most potent reasons for eternal torment come from the book of Revelation. According to Robert Peterson (The Case for Traditional values, 160), the third angel's message is one of the three "most revealing biblical establishments on hell." Like many others, he reckons that these verses teach that hell results in eternal conscious torment for the lost. If their smoke goes up forever, then the unsaved must burn forever.

CHAPTER 1
TORMENT IN THE PRESENCE OF THE LAMB

Revelation 14:10 says that the worshipers of the beast "will be tormented in the presence of the holy angels and the presence of the Lamb." It means that the Lamb and his angels will watch them in hell. God gave Christ "authority to execute judgment" (John 5:27), which is what he will do. "The end" will surely come "when he has eliminated all rule and all authority and power" (1 Cor 15:24). Jesus has the keys to the kingdom of heaven and hell.

Its flows will turn into terrain, its loose earth into brimstone, and its land will become burning terrain. It will not be quenched night or day; Its smoke will last forever. From generation to generation, it will be desolate. (Isaiah 34:9).

Babylon's smoke also goes up forever.

In Revelation 17, the harlot named Babylon sits on a scarlet beast (Rev 17:5, 3). She is a symbol of false religion that has ruled over the kings of the world for ages, with the weight of false Christianity. (Traders or Babylon the great.) The beast on which she sits symbolizes the rulers of the world.

The third angel, Revelation 19:3, prophesies that *"the smoke from her (Babylon) goes up forever and ever."* But, for a minimum of three reasons, mean that she will be tormented forever:

- Firstly, Babylon is not a spiritual being that can be tormented. *Babylon is a symbol of false religion.*

- Secondly, false religion will not always exist. When Christ returns, all remnants of false religion will be destroyed. He who sits on the throne said: *"Behold, I am making all things new"* (Rev 21:5).

- Thirdly, we are distinctly told that Babylon will be destroyed:

"The great city of Babylon will be thrown down, never to be found again" (Rev 18:21). And "The beast will hate the harlot and will make her unhappy and naked and will eat her flesh and will burn her up with fire" (Rev 17:16).

- Since Babylon will be destroyed, the ever-rising smoke shows destruction. The ever-rising smoke from the torment of the beast's followers in the warning of the third angel stands that they will be destroyed.

God's people will live *"forever and ever,"* but all that will remain of the people who accepted the mark of the beast is smoke, the memory of their horrible fate.

The horrific destruction of the dead, whom God and His people love, will be gone.

The winepress of the wrath of God

The third angel warns the people of the world that the beast's followers *"will drink of the wine of the wrath of God"* (Rev 14:10). These verses do not define the people drinking that wine. After some further warnings (Rev 14:12-13), the last part of Revelation 14,

- Which establishes the return of Christ (Rev 14:14)

- Does define the outpouring of God's wrath:

- At his return, the people with the mark of the beast indicated by "the vine of the earth" (Rev 14:19),

- Will be thrown "into the great wine press of the wrath of God" (Rev 14:19).

- "And the wine press was flattened outside the city, and blood flowed from the wine press, as high as a horse's bridle, for about two hundred miles" (Rev 14:20).

- The setting demands that the wine press, which refers to Christ's return, "the wrath of God," which the third angel warns about.

The traditional eternal torment reading of the angel's warning has tension between the eternal torment expected in Revelation 14:11 and the picture of the final destruction that follows at the return of Christ (Rev 14:14-20).

But if Revelation 14:11 is explained as eternal destruction, then there is no tension between the third angel's warning of final judgment (Rev 14:9-11) and the explanation of final judgment in Revelation 14:14- 20.

The Seven Last Plagues

The seven last plagues are called "the last because in them the wrath of God is finished" (Rev 15:1).

The wrath of God, which the third angel warned (Rev 14:10), will be finished during the seven last plagues. These seven last plagues are poured out in Revelation 16. The following two chapters break the flow of events.

The seventh plague continues in Revelation 19 (Rev 16:19 and 19:2), ending in another type of the return of Christ (Rev 19:11), which also mentions *"the wine press of the fierce wrath of God"* (Rev 19:15), which we saw at the end of Revelation 14. Since the seven last plagues terminate in Christ's return, and *because in them the wrath of God is finished,"* it is determined that *"the wine press of the fierce wrath of God,"* which represents the destruction of the lost at the return of Christ (Rev 19:21), is the wrath of God which the second angel warned about (Rev 14:10-11). As said in the report of his return in Revelation 19: The rest were killed with the sword which came from the mouth of Jesus who sat on the horse, and all the birds were filled with their flesh. (Rev 19:21). The ever-rising smoke in the third angel's message shows permanent destruction.

The lake of fire is the second death (Rev 20:10) and is destruction.

The series:

- Death,

- Eternal Life,

- Eternal Torment.

And the devil who deceived them was thrown into the lake of fire and brimstone, where the beast and the false prophet are also; and they will be tormented day and night forever and ever. (Rev 20:10, NKJV).

Revelation 20:10 has all the essential constituents for the accepted doctrine of eternal torment: the lake of fire, conscious suffering, and infinite time. And the lost are also thrown into the lake of fire: If anyone's name was not found written in the *Book of Life*, they were thrown into the lake of fire" (Rev 20:15).

According to Revelation 20:10, the devil, the beast, and the false prophets will be tormented in the lake of fire forever and ever. It shows that Revelation 20:10 is a representative explanation of eternal destruction:

CHAPTER 2
THE BOOK OF REVELATION (PART I)

After death is thrown into the lake of fire, nobody else will die (Rev 21:4). Revelation defines the lake of fire as the second death, the final and permanent death. The beast and the false prophet are spiritual beings that can suffer eternal torment. Revelation said plainly that the beast would be destroyed. If neutral or company of beings, such as death, the beast, and the false prophet, can be thrown into the lake of fire to be destroyed, then Satan will also be consumed when he is thrown into it.

Revelation 20:10 is an event at the end of the Millennium. One thousand years earlier, at Christ's return, the beast and the false prophet were captured and "thrown alive into the lake of fire which burns with brimstone" (Rev 19:20). At the same time, all sinners are put to death (Rev 19:21). At the end of the Millennium, all sinners that ever lived, "the dead did not live again until the thousand years is finished. (Rev 20:5), now when the thousands years have terminated, Satan will be released from his prison and will go out to the nations which are in the four corners of the earth, Gog and Magog, to gather them together to battle, whose number is as the sands of the sea deceived by Satan (Rev 20:8), surround "the camp of the saints" but "fire came down from God out of heaven and devoured them" (Rev 20:9). Then the devil, which is another name for Satan (Rev 20:2), "was thrown into the lake of fire," where the beast and false prophet are (Rev 20:10).

Book of Revelation (Part II)

Consider the three spiritual beings in the lake of fire (Rev 20:10):

- The beast has seven heads and ten horns and appears from the sea (Rev 13:1).

- The false prophet is also a beast, but it comes "up out of the earth" and has "two horns like a lamb" (Rev 13:11).

- Satan is termed as a dragon (Rev 12:9) that also has seven heads and ten horns (Rev 12:3) and hunts a woman (Rev 12:6, 14) who stands on the moon (Rev 12:1).

- The harlot of Babylon sits on the beast (Rev 17:3), but she also sits on "many waters" (Rev 17:1) and on "seven mountains" (Rev 17:9).

Death is also thrown into the Lake of Fire.

At the end of Revelation 20, after the final judgment (Rev 20:11-12), "death and hades were thrown into the lake of fire" (Rev 20:14). Hades is the place where the dead are. The fourth seal shows death and hades and says that hades follow death (Rev 7:8). If something like death can be thrown into the lake of fire, it is a place of conscious suffering. Revelation explains this: "There will no longer be any death" (Rev 21:4). If throwing death into the lake of fire is the destruction of death, then throwing other things into the lake of fire also means that they are destroyed.

The Lake of Fire is the Second Death.

However, Revelation explains its symbols. For example, the "many waters" on which the harlot sits (Rev 17:1) are described as "peoples and multitudes and nations and tongues" (Rev 17:15). The lake of fire is also distinctly explained; not once but twice, namely as "the second death: *This is the second death, the lake of fire*" (Rev 20:14). "The lake that burns with fire and brimstone, which is **the second death**" (Rev 21:8). Explaining the lake of fire as "the second death" means that the second death is different from the first death.

All dead people will be resurrected from the first death (Rev 20:5; John 5:28-29), but the worshipers of the beast will die three times:

- When Christ returns, or earlier, they die for the first time (Rev 19:21).

- At the end of the Millennium, fire from heaven devours them (Rev 20:9).

- For that reason, it is "the dead" who stands before the throne (Rev 20:12).

Just like the souls "underneath the altar" figuratively cry out for revenge (Rev 6:10) but symbolize God's awareness of the injustice suffered by his people and his intention to revenge their deaths, the dead figuratively stand before the throne of God to be judged.

Then, once the angels of the universe have verified from the records that God's judgments are perfect (Rev 20:12), "death and Hades were thrown into the lake of fire. This is the **second death**, the lake of fire." (Rev 20:14) A person may die the first death any number of times. Over history, many people were resurrected from death but died the first death a second time. But a person dies the second death only once. Once a soul has been cast into the lake of fire, which is the second death, he is never again seen doing anything.

The beast and the false prophet "were thrown alive into the lake of fire" when Christ returned (Rev 19:11). Later, they never again do anything in Revelation. The devil is cast into the lake of fire one thousand years later (Rev 20:10) and is never heard of again. The same applies to the people with the mark of the beast, who are cast into the lake of fire after the judgment (Rev 20:15; cf. 20:11). The second death is when they are thrown into the lake of fire. It is the final and permanent death. From "the second death," there will be no resurrection.

Satan will also be defeated.

The devil is cast into the lake of fire with the beast and the false prophet (Rev 20:10). He is a spiritual being and may suffer everlasting torment. But the company of beings, such as death, the beast, and the false prophet, can be thrown into the lake of fire to be destroyed, and then the lake of fire metaphorically consumes everything thrown into it. Therefore, when Satan is thrown into that lake, he is also eradicated.

Ezekiel 28 describes Satan, for it talks about an "anointed cherub who covers" (Eze 28:14), "You were blameless in your ways … until unrighteousness was found in you" (Eze 28:15). "Your heart was lifted because of your beauty" (Eze 28:17). Therefore, God judged him. "He consumed him with fire, turned him to ashes" (Eze 28:18). "You will cease to be forever" (Eze 28:19).

Why this horrible representation?

I suggest that Judgment Day uses the phrase "tormented day and night forever and ever" because the utter destruction of people who have been created in God's image is genuinely horrifying, both for God and for people who think like Him (Rev 14:1). Think of the people around you. Every one of them is a miracle. To lose even one person is an eternal tragedy. Therefore, God paints a genuinely frightening and astonishing picture of the end of the people who accept the mark of the beast.

The Book of Revelation (Part III)

The second death is the final and irreversible death. From the second death, there will be no resurrection.

- The Beast is an extension of the beasts of Daniel.

- The three seven-headed beasts in Revelation (Rev 12:3; 13:1; 17:3) are a single beast with three bodies and seven heads.

- The beast will be destroyed.

- Satan will also be destroyed.

- The utter destruction of people who have been created in God's image is genuinely horrifying, both for God and for people who think like Him.

God will ultimately put the wicked out of existence, leaving only the righteous to live on in immortality. (Rev 14:9-11; 20:10). The third angel's warning symbolizes eternal destruction. Satan will be defeated in the lake of fire. The purpose is for eternal torment.

The Rich Man and Lazarus

Jesus told the story of a rich man who lived joyously in splendor every day and a poor man named Lazarus who lay at his gate, covered with sores (Luke 16:19-20). Both men died. The angels carried away the poor man to Abraham's bosom. The rich man "was buried." "In Hades he lifted his eyes, being in torment, and saw Abraham far away and Lazarus in his bosom" (Luke 16:22-23).

The rich man pleaded with Abraham that Lazarus would bring him water, "for I am in pain in this flame." Abraham then gave two reasons to refuse this request:

- Firstly, while the rich man, during his life, had "good things," Lazarus had "bad things." But Lazarus is "now … being comforted here," while the rich man is "in pain."

- Secondly, between the places where Lazarus and the rich man are, "there is a great gap … so that … none may cross over." (Luke 16:24-26)

The rich man then begged Abraham to send Lazarus to his five brothers. He said, "if someone goes to them from the dead, they will repent" (Luke 16:27-30). But Abraham responded: "If they do not listen to Moses and the Prophets, they will not be persuaded even if someone rises from the dead" (Luke 16:31).

Why does this prove Eternal Torment?

Firstly, the main point of this story is contained in verse 31, namely that only "Moses and the Prophets" can lead people to repentance. That is how parables work; Jesus told a parable to communicate a single message. In this case, Jesus explains about the afterlife. He was telling His audience what would happen when they die.

While they are dead, their bodies have decayed, and they are souls that live as spirit beings; Lazarus and the rich man still have eyes, fingers, and tongues (Luke 16:23, 24) and a physical "opening" between them.

Since these things are to be taken clearly, the rich man's agony "in this flame" must also be taken as real suffering.

- This story is about Hades; it is about Hell.

- Secondly, the rich man is "in hades" (Luke 16:23). This term refers to the grave, the state of death, or the transitional state. In Greek mythology, it refers to the underworld. According to Revelation 20, at the end of the Millennium, after the lost have been put to death (Rev 20:9) and after the grand final judgment (Rev 20:11-12).

- "Hades were thrown into the lake of fire" (Rev 20:14). Hades is the temporary place where the dead are kept until the final destruction. (Gehenna); the area of the ultimate destruction of the lost (Matt 10:28).

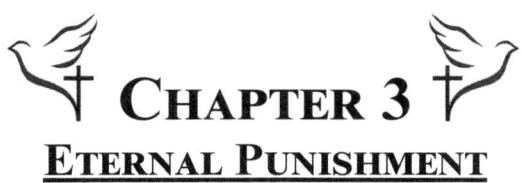

CHAPTER 3
ETERNAL PUNISHMENT

Eternal torment is the fact that the Bible describes the state of the lost with "eternal punishment" and "the eternal fire." For example, Jesus said: Then He will also say to those on His left, depart from me, doomed ones, into the eternal fire. These will go away into eternal punishment, but the righteous into eternal life" (Matt 25:41, 46). Eternal torment is hell.

Eternal Fire

However, Jude uses *"Sodom and Gomorrah"* as "an example" of "the punishment of eternal fire" (Jude 1:7) of those who "deny our only Lord, Jesus Christ" (Jude 1:5). That fire destroyed Sodom and Gomorrah but has gone out long since. These events are transcribed in Genesis 19:24-28. The Lord rained brimstone and fire upon Sodom and Gomorrah from the Lord out of heaven. The smoke went up like the smoke of a furnace. But today, the fire is burning in hell. If that is what "eternal fire" did to Sodom and Gomorrah, then we should assume that the "eternal fire," Jesus mentioned, will be lost forever.

Eternal Punishment

We should also accept the "eternal punishment" Jesus mentioned in Matthew 25, eternal torment. Torment is one kind of punishment, but it is the only thing that could be called punishment. The Bible refers to *"eternal torment"* or *"eternal suffering."* Another form of punishment is destruction. Paul wrote, "Those who do not know God will pay the penalty of eternal destruction" (2 Thess 1:8-9). It is "eternal punishment," such as destruction. (2 Thessalonians 1:8-9) When the Lord Jesus is revealed from heaven with His mighty angels in flaming fire, dealing out justice to those who do not know God,

These will pay the penalty of eternal destruction, away from the Lord's presence and His power's glory, when He is glorified with his saints on that day.

Destruction is an eternal process.

Since destruction is an *"eternal"* process, if "eternal" describes the consequence of the action of destruction, then that destruction is "eternal destruction." If the person has been destroyed (defeated), he no longer exists.

And shut out from the presence of the Lord.

The destruction is by noting that "those who do not know God will pay the penalty of eternal destruction, away from the presence of the Lord." However, *"eternal destruction"* and *"shut* out from the presence of the Lord" are two things the lost suffer. Then, "shut out from the presence of the Lord" means they will not dwell with the Lord.

However, the lost will be tormented eternally. That verse reads as follows: Many of those who sleep in the dust of the ground will awaken first, the dead in Christ to everlasting life, those alive will be caught up in the rapture, but the others to disgrace and endless scorn. (Daniel 12: 2). The lost to experience "disgrace and everlasting scorn" requires that they will always exist and be aware of their condition, the *"everlasting life"* of the righteous.

Isaiah 66 shows that the person's shame and scorn will continue to exist after the person has been demolished because those who will receive "everlasting life" will think of the lost with contempt.

- First, *"the Lord will come in fire … to deliver his anger with fury* ... and those slain by the Lord shall be many" (Isa 66:15-16).

- It is Revelation 19:21, which says that the lost will be put to death when Christ returns.

- Next, Isaiah 66 mentions *"the new heavens and the new earth"* (Isa 66:22), which is also mentioned in Revelation (Rev 21:1).

- It shows what Isaiah describes in the following verses are the conditions in eternity (Daniel 12:2).

Then, in "The new heavens and the new earth," the saved: "will … look on the corpses of the men. Who have sinned against Me. For their worm will not die and their fire will not be quenched; and they will be a loathing to all mankind" (Isa 66:24). What has happened to the lost? They are dead. The word "disgust" is "disapproval" in Daniel 12:2; dragon. Isaiah shows that the saved will think of the lost with "disgrace and everlasting disapproval" (Dan 12:2).

Both God and God's people will be sorrowful over the loss. It will not be dislike for the lost but horror when they think of what sin has done to the people they loved. Their worm does not die, and the fire is not quenched. (Mark 9).

Jesus said: "If your hand causes you to stumble, cut it off; you should enter life crippled, then, having your two hands, to go into hell, into the unquenchable fire, where their worm does not die, and the fire is not quenched." (Mark 9:43-44; Matt 18:8-9). Then they will look on the corpses of the men who have transgressed against Me. Their worm will not die, their fire will not be quenched, and they will be loathing to all humanity.(Isa 66:24).

CHAPTER 4
THE GOVERNMENT OF THE PROMISED SON

In **Isaiah 9:16,** "For the leaders of this people cause them to error; and they that are led of them are ruined."

The intensified wickedness of Israel extended to all classes, even the fatherless and widows" who often were the objects of special mercy. Israel was led into idolatry by their spiritual leaders and civil leaders. They even mixed pagan rituals with their worship of God. Jeroboam included worship of the calf. Those of Judah had not slipped that far but were guilty themselves to a lesser degree.

"Woe be unto the pastors": These false leaders failed to assure the people's welfare. They are starting with the kings, other civil heads, prophets, and priests. They stood in utter difference to the shepherds God would later give the nation. Other significant chapters which condemn evil shepherds and false prophets include (Jeremiah 14, 27, 28; Isa. 28; Ezek. 13, 34; Micah 3; and Zech. 11).

Jeremiah 23:1: "Woe be unto the pastors that destroy and scatter the sheep of my pasture! Said the Lord."

The shepherd is a typical representation of Israel's civil and spiritual leaders (Psalm 78:70-72; Ezek.34). But these leaders have destroyed their flocks rather than protecting and meeting their needs. In an earlier example, we decided these pastors meant the same thing as shepherds. The word Fermented wine is a false teaching.

The false shepherd has no regard for the sheep, whether then or now. They are interested only in their welfare.

I believe this Scripture speaks to the leaders of the people then and the leaders in our churches today.

- These false shepherds do; they scatter and destroy the sheep.

Jeremiah 23:2: "Therefore thus saith the Lord God of Israel against the pastors that feed my people; Ye have scattered my flock, and driven them away, and have not visited them: behold, I will visit upon you the evil of your doings, saith the Lord."

"O ye shepherds" or "governors" and civil leaders, as the Targum. The civil rulers, magistrates, kings, and princes of the land of Israel. Since ecclesiastical rulers, priests, and prophets are mentioned as distinct from them in (Jer. 23:9). Whose business it was to rule, guide, protect, and defend the people. But, instead of that, they were such. "That destroy and scatter the sheep of my pasture, saith the Lord God": Set them bad examples and led them into idolatry and other sins, which were the cause of their ruin and of their being carried captive and scattered in other countries. And their sin was more aggravated since these people were the Lord's pasture sheep. Whom he had an interest in and regard unto and had committed them to the care and charge of these pastors, governors, and civil leaders to be taken care of.

The food here is the Word of God. It is imperative to bring the Word of God in absolute truth. Most of the people are seriously influenced by the message the shepherd brings. If the good news is correct, it brings the Lord life, health, and joy. If the statement they get is untrue, it brings death to the body and soul.

The statement "Lord God of Israel" tells us that the crime against the evil shepherd is a false religion. Israel did not have many gods. **The Lord God is their only God.** It is true of the Jewish nation, physical Israel, and all believers in Christ. The leaders had scattered the people to the foreign lands with false worship.

"I will gather": God pledged to restore exiled Israelites to their ancient soil (Jeremiah 30 to 33, and 16:14-15). The land in view was Palestine, being compared with all the other countries, thus assuring

that the regathering would be as exact as the scattering.

The restoration of Judah from Babylon referred to a language that, in its fullness, can only refer to the final restoration of God's people "out of all the countries" under the Messiah.

"Nor will any be missing" shows that no one will be missing or detached. These are prophecies not yet fulfilled (Jeremiah 32:37-38; Isa. 60:21; Ezek. 34:11-16).

The Spiritual decline of the seven churches (Rev.2 and 3) also argues for the later date. Those churches were strong and spiritually healthy in the mid-60s when Paul last ministered in Asia Minor. The brief time between Paul's ministry there and the end of Nero's reign was too short for such a decline to have occurred. The longer time gap also explains the rise of the heretical sect known as the Nicolaitans (2:6, 15), not mentioned in Paul's letters, not even to one or more of these same churches (Ephesians).

Finally, dating Revelation during Nero's reign does not allow time for John's ministry in Asia Minor to reach the point at which the authorities would have felt the need to exile him.

Revelation seventeen returns and fills in some of what happened during the Tribulation. In Revelation 16, the Great Tribulation ended. Now Revelation seventeen covers when Babylon the Harlot or the Religious Babylon is Destroyed ("Babylon the Harlot"). Archaeologists tell us that Babylon is the cradle of civilization. Located on the Euphrates River's shores, this city's ruins have revealed some of the most ancient documents of past generations.

The city, begun by Nimrod, a rebel before the Lord, authored some of the greatest evils ever to fall on humanity. However, two of these evils will be destroyed during the Tribulation period. Revelation seventeen is the destruction of religious Babylon that occurs about the center of the seven years after the Antichrist declares himself to be God and no longer needs the One World Religion.

In Revelation eighteen, we will read about the destruction of the commercial, political Babylon when it takes place at the end of the

Great Tribulation. In ancient days, Satan made Babylon the capital of this evil operation.

From this headquarters was started false religion, humanity's attempt for self-government in defiance of God's will, and city dwellings for commercial and social purposes contrary to God's command to "be fruitful and increase in number and fill the earth" (Gen. 1:28).

These great evils, which have damned the souls of millions by substituting counterfeit solutions to natural human problems that would ordinarily lead a person to God, will all be destroyed at the end of the Tribulation period. It describes the coming judgment of God on the religious system that has enslaved humanity in superstitious darkness for centuries.

The woman is a great city: "*The woman you saw is the great city* that rules over the kings of the earth" (Rev. 17:18). Many have taken this to mean that the woman is the capital city of Antichrist's kingdom, but this cannot be, for Antichrist himself rules over the kings of the earth.

If *the woman is not the Antichrist*, what other possible explanation can we have for such united world dominance? The only answer is the one system before which all kings, dictators, and nations were forced to bow down throughout history, that is, the Babylonian religion of idolatry. One cannot go anywhere in the world without being confronted with idolatry.

No system in history has enslaved more people than this awful religion. It should not take us by surprise that this prostitute woman, the religious system, is referred to as a city. When used symbolically, a woman is always projected to signify a spiritual or religious movement throughout the Scripture. If a good woman, it is *"Jehovah's wife"* or "the bride of Christ." If an evil woman, such as "a prostitute," it is the corrupt religious system of idolatry.

Since the woman who rides the beast gets her authority from the beast, the Holy Spirit uses this description to show how religious Babylon and governmental Babylon are intertwined. However, they are devastated at different times. The prostitute's spiritual Babylon is destroyed by the "beast and the kings of the earth," who "hate the prostitute" and kill her.

It clears the way for the Antichrist to fulfill the lifetime dream of Satan to get people to worship him. The woman is ruined in the middle of the tribulation; the governmental system will be destroyed at the end when commercial and political Babylon. (Rev. 18).

With *"Mystery Babylon, the mother of Prostitutes"* out of the way, "all inhabitants of the earth will worship the beast, all whose names are not written in the book of life belonging to the Lamb that was slain from the creation of the world" (Rev. 13:8).

The Vision of the Woman

Ten details describe this woman:

- The great prostitute.

- Who sits on many waters?

- With her, the kings of the earth committed adultery.

- The inhabitants of the world were intoxicated with the wine of her adulteries.

- A woman sitting on a scarlet beast.

- Dressed in purple and scarlet.

- Glittering with gold, precious stones, and pearls.

- She held a golden cup filled with abominable things and the filth of her adulteries.

- On her forehead: Mystery Babylon the Great, the mother of Prostitutes and the Abomination of the Earth.

- Drunk with the blood of the saints, the blood of those who bore testimony to Jesus.

Even before we come to the angel's interpretation of this vision, we are not dealing with a mere human being, for no one woman can commit fornication with the kings of the earth, nor can a woman be *"drunk with the blood of the saints,* the blood of those who bore testimony to Jesus."

Revelations seventeen and eighteen picture the judgment of God on a system, empire, or city called Babylon the Great (17:5); it is a more detailed description of the seventh vial (16:17).

The *"great whore,* is named **"BABYLON THE GREAT."** Her "judgment." The *"waters"* represent the various peoples and nations of the earth. She "sits upon" them in the sense that she has worldwide influence. Her harlotry and "fornication" refer either to physical immorality or spiritual adultery. Idolatry and religious apostasy (Isa. 1:21; 23:16-17; Jer. 2:20-37; 13:27; Ezek. 16:15-43; Hosea 2:5; Nahum 3:4).

The "kings" and "inhabitants of the earth" have opened their arms to her influence. The "beast" is the first Beast of chapter 13, the Antichrist, and his empire. Her sitting upon the Beast is the intimate association between the Antichrist and the harlot, an association of support, influence, or control.

And there came one of the seven angels which had the seven vials, and talked with me, saying unto me, come here; I will show unto thee the judgment of the great whore that sits upon many glasses of water (Revelation 17:1).

"Seven angels":

- The reference to these angels' links to Revelation seventeen and eighteen with the vial (bowl)

- Judgments extend to Christ's second coming (Revelation 16:17).

- Revelations seventeen and eighteen put attention to one aspect of those vial judgments: the verdict of Babylon.

- The decisions already described affect the final world system.

"Great whore" (Revelation 14:8).

- Prostitution often symbolizes idolatry or religious apostasy (Jer. 3:6-9; Ezek. 16:3; 20:30; Hosea 4:15; 5:3; 6:10; 9:1). Nineveh (Nahum 3:1, 4)

- Tyre (Isa. 23:17),

- Even Jerusalem (Isa. 1:21) is a harlot city.

"Sits on many waters": The picture emphasizes the sovereign power of the harlot. The image of a ruler seated on a throne, ruling the waters, symbolizing the world's nations.

The "whore" here is not a literal woman. In Hosea, his wife, who was a whore, was speaking of Israel. Here, this "whore" is speaking of the idolatrous church. The statement *"sits upon many waters"* is large groups of people. They are not the true church nor the apostate church. God calls it the harlot church, which is not faithful to God and worldly.

While claiming to be Christian, this church finds many reasons to conform to the beast and the evil world system. They will be the one-world religion appearing after the church saints have been raptured ("One World Order").

However, without question, the church has compromised with the world and is no longer a pure virgin in the sight of God. I genuinely believe that many churches fall into this category today. Worldliness has crept into our churches. The sad thing is that if she would repent, God would take her back, but she would not.

The Bride of Christ is called a city, the part of the church that has not compromised. The other opposite side of that is the harlot. It is also called a city but is evil because of compromise.

This is not only the apostate church in Rome but the apostate in many other churches. Again, the waters tell us this apostate church is throughout the masses.

CHAPTER 5

THE QUARREL BETWEEN SATAN AND THE PRINCE OF HELL

There was a disagreement between Satan and the Prince of hell concerning the expected arrival of Christ in hell. While all the saints were rejoicing, behold Satan, the prince, and captain of death, said to the prince of hell, prepare to receive Jesus of Nazareth himself, who boasted that he was the Son of God; and yet was a man afraid of death, and said, my soul is sorrowful even to death.

Besides, he did many injuries to me and many others; for those whom I made blind, lame, and those also whom I tormented with several devils, he cured by the word of God; yea, and those whom I brought dead to thee, he by force takes away from thee.

To this, the prince of hell replied to Satan, who is that so powerful prince, and yet a man afraid of death? All the people of the earth are subject to my power, whom thou brought to subjection by my authority. But if he is so powerful in human form, I insist to you for the truth that he is almighty in his divine form, and no man can resist his power.

Therefore, when he said he was afraid of death, he designed to trap you, and it will be unhappy for you for everlasting ages. Then Satan, replying, spoke to the prince of hell, why did you express doubt and was afraid to receive that Jesus of Nazareth, both thy adversary and mine?

As for me, I tempted him and stirred up my old people, the Jews, with enthusiasm and anger against him. I sharpened the spear for his suffering, mixed with gall and vinegar, and commanded that he should drink it; they prepared the cross to crucify him, and the nails to pierce through his hands and feet; and now his death is near at hand, I will bring him here, subject both to you and me. Then the prince of hell answered, said, you said to me just now that he took away the dead from me by force. They who kept here till they should live again upon earth were taken away not by their power but by prayers made to God, and their almighty God took them from me. (The Lost Books of the Bible, Nicodemus, Pg.82- 88,1926).

Who then is that Jesus of Nazareth that by his word has taken away the dead from me without prayer to God? Perhaps it is the same who took away from me Lazarus after he had been dead four days, and did both stink and was rotted, and of whom I had possession as a deceased person, yet he brought him to life again by his power.

Satan answered, saying to the prince of hell, it is the same person, Jesus of Nazareth. When the prince of hell heard this, he said to him, "I order you by the powers which belong to you and me, that you bring him not here to me. When I heard the force of his word, I trembled for fear, and all my wicked company was simultaneously frightened.

And we could not detain Lazarus, but he gave himself a shake, and with all the hatred, he at once went away from us; the very earth in which the dead body of Lazarus was impacted presently turned him out alive.

And I know now that he is Almighty God who could perform such things, mighty in his dominion, and mighty in his human form, who is the Savior of humanity. Bring not, therefore, this person Jesus of Nazareth here. For he will set at liberty all I hold in prison under unbelief, bound with restraints of their sins, and will charge them to everlasting life. (The Lost Books of the Bible, Nicodemus, Pg.82- 88,1926).

CHAPTER 6
JESUS ARRIVED AT HELL GATES

Jesus arrives at hell gates, there is confusion, and he descends into hell. He holds the keys to Heaven and Hell.

And while Satan and the prince of hell were conversing with each other, unexpectedly, there was a voice as of thunder and rushing of winds, saying, "Lift your heads, O' you gate! And be lifted, you gate of hell, you everlasting gate, and the King of Glory shall come in. (Psalm 24:7).

When the princes of hell heard this, he said to Satan, leave from me and begone out of my residence. If you are a mighty warrior, fight with the King of Glory. But what do you have to do with him?

And he cast him forth from his dwellings. And the prince of hell said to his wicked officers, Shut the brass gates of cruelty, fasten them with iron bars, and fight fearlessly, in case we become captives.

But when the entire assembly of saints heard this, they spoke with a loud voice of anger to the prince of hell. Open the gates that the King of Glory may come in. And the divine prophet David cried out, saying, did not I when on earth genuinely prophesy and say, O those men would praise the Lord for his goodness and his wonderful works to the children of men.

He has broken the brass gates and cut the iron bars in pieces. He has taken them because of their iniquity and unrighteousness, and they are grief-stricken. After this, holy Isaiah, another prophet, spoke to all the saints, did not I rightly prophesy to you when I was alive on earth? The dead men shall live, rise again who are in their graves, and rejoice who are in the earth; for the dew from the Lord shall bring deliverance to them.

And I said in another place, O' death, where is thy victory? O' death, where is thy sting? When all the saints heard these things spoken by Isaiah, they said to the prince of hell, Open now the gates, and take away the iron bars; for you will now be bound and have no power. (The Lost Books of the Bible, Nicodemus, Pg.82-88,1926).

Then there was a great voice, as the sound of thunder said, lift your heads, O' you gate and be lifted up, you gate of hell, and the King of Glory will enter. The prince of hell, recognizing the same voice repeated, cried out as though he had been ignorant: who is the King of Glory?

David replied to the prince of hell and said, "I understand the words of that voice because I spoke to them by his spirit. And now, as I have said above, I say unto you, The Lord strong and mighty, the Lord mighty in battle: he is the King of Glory, and he is the Lord in heaven and earth. (Psalm 24:8).

He has looked down to hear the groans of the prisoners and to set loose those appointed to death. And now, you filthy and stinking prince of hell, open the gates; the King of Glory may enter, for he is the Lord of heaven and earth.

While David was saying this, the mighty Lord appeared as a man and lightened those places which had ever before been in darkness. And broke in pieces the fetters which before could not be broken; and with his invincible power visited those who set in the deep night by iniquity and the shadow of death by sin. (The Lost Books of the Bible, Nicodemus, Pg.82- 88,1926).

CHAPTER 7

DEATH AND THE DEMONS IN GREAT HORROR AT JESUS COMING

Death and the devils are horrified at Jesus's Coming, and he tramples on end, seizes the Prince of Hell, and takes Adam and saints to heaven. Not showing respect for death and her cruel officers hearing these things were captured with fear in their several kingdoms in hell when they saw the clearness of the light. And Jesus himself suddenly appeared in their habitations; they cried out and said you bind us; you seem to expect our confusion before the Lord.

Who are you, who has no sign of corruption but that bright presence, which is complete proof of your greatness, yet you seem to take no notice? Who are you, so powerful and so weak, so great and so little a man and yet a soldier of the first; who can command in the form of a servant as a common soldier? The King of Glory, dead and alive though once slain on the cross.

Who laid dead in the grave and have come down alive to us, and in your death and your death, all creatures trembled, and the stars were moved and now has your freedom among the dead, and given the disruption to our legions? Who are you? Who releases the captives held in chains by original sin and brings them into their former freedom. Who are you, who spreads such glorious and divine light over those who were made blind by the darkness of sin?

In like manner, all the legions of demons were apprehended with horror and, with the most submissive fear, cried out and said, why come here, O' Jesus, that you are a man so powerful and glorious in majesty, so bright as to have no spot, and so pure as to have no crime. For that lower world of earth, which was always till now subject to us, and from which was ever till now subject us, and from which we received tribute. Never send us such presents as these to the princes of hell. (The Lost Books of the Bible, Nicodemus, Pg.82-88,1926).

Who are you, with such courage, who enter among our dwellings and are not only not afraid to threaten us with the most significant punishments but also try to rescue all others from the chains in which we hold them? Perhaps you are that Jesus, who Satan just now spoke to our prince about, that by the death of the cross, you were about to receive the power of death. Then the King of Glory tread on death seized the prince of hell, removed him from all his might, and took our earthly father Adam with him to his glory.(The Lost Books of the Bible, Nicodemus, Pg.82- 88,1926).

CHAPTER 8
BEELZEBUB, PRINCE OF HELL

Beelzebub rebukes Satan for persecuting Jesus and bringing him to hell. Jesus forever gives Beelzebub dominion over Satan as payment for taking away Adam and his sons.

Then the prince of hell took Satan and, with great indignation, said to him, O you prince of destruction, author of Beelzebub's defeat and banishment, the scorn of God's angels and loathed by all righteous persons! What inclined thee to act thus?

You would crucify the King of Glory and, by his destruction, have promised us considerable advantages, but as a fool, you were ignorant of what you were about. For behold now that Jesus of Nazareth, with the brightness of his glorious divinity, puts all the horrid powers of darkness and death to flight.

He has broken down our prisons from top to bottom, dismissed all the captives, released all who were bound, and all who were wont formerly to groan under the weight of their torments have now insulted us, and we are likely to be defeated by their prayers.

Our wicked dominions were submissive; no part of humanity is now left in our subjection, but on the other hand, they all boldly defy us. Before, the dead never behaved disrespectfully towards us, nor could prisoners ever be merry on any occasion. (The Lost Books of the Bible, Nicodemus, Pg.82- 88,1926).

O Satan, thou prince of all wicked, father of the wicked and abandoned, why would you attempt this deed, seeing our prisoners were previously always without minor hopes of salvation and life?

But now, not one of them ever groans, nor is there the slightest appearance of a tear on any of their faces. O prince Satan, you great keeper of the hell regions, all thy advantages which you did acquire by the forbidden tree, and the loss of Paradise, you have now lost the wood of the cross. And thy happiness stopped when you crucified Jesus Christ the King of Glory.

You have acted against thine own interest and mine as you will presently perceive by those large torments and unlimited punishments you are about to suffer. O Satan, prince of all evil, author of death, and source of all pride, you should first have inquired into the vicious crimes of Jesus of Nazareth, and then you would have found that he was guilty of no-fault worthy of death.

Why did you venture without either reason or justice to crucify him and bring down to our region's person innocent and righteous and thereby lose all sinners, wicked and unrighteous people in the world? While the prince of hell was thus speaking to Satan, the King of Glory said to Beelzebub, the prince of hell, Satan, the prince shall be subject to thy dominion forever, in the room of Adam and his righteous sons, who are mine.(The Lost Books of the Bible, Nicodemus, Pg.82-88,1926).

CHAPTER 9

JESUS TAKES ADAM AND THE SAINTS TO PARADISE

Christ takes Adam by the hand, the rest of the saints join hands, and they all ascend with him to Paradise. Then Jesus stretched forth his hand and said, come to me, all my saints who created in my image, condemned by the tree of forbidden fruit, the devil, and death. Live now by the wood of my cross; the devil, the prince of this world, is overcome, and death is conquered.

Then presently, all the saints were joined under the hand of the highest God, and the Lord Jesus laid hold on Adam's hand and said to him, Peace be to thee, and all thy righteous future generations, which is mine. Then Adam, casting himself at the feet of Jesus, addressed him, with tears, in humble language, and a loud voice, saying, I will praise thee, O Lord, for you have lifted me, and has not made my enemies rejoice over me. O Lord my God, I cried, and you have healed me.

O Lord, you have brought up my soul from the grave; you have kept me alive, that I should not go down to the pit. Sing unto the Lord, all you saints of his, and give thanks at the remembrance of his holiness. For his anger endures but for a moment; in his favor is life.

In like manner, all saints, prostrate at the feet of Jesus, said with one voice, your art come, O redeemer of the world, and have carried out all things, which you did foretell by the law and thy holy prophets. You have redeemed the living by the cross, and art comes down to us, that by the cross's death, you mightiest deliver us from hell, and by thy power from the end. (The Lost Books of the Bible, Nicodemus, Pg.82-88,1926).

☩Chapter 10☩
Jesus Delivers Adam to Michael the Archangel

The Blessed Thief Story.

They meet Enoch and Elijah in heaven and the blessed thief, who relates how he came to paradise. Then, the Lord held Adam by the hand and delivered him to Michael, the archangel, and he led them into Paradise, filled with mercy and glory. And two very ancient men met them and were asked by the saints, who are you, who have not yet been with us in hell and have had your bodies placed in paradise?

One of them answered I am Enoch, translated by the word of God, and this man with me is Elijah the Tishbite, translated in a fiery chariot.

Here we have been and have not tasted death but are now about to return at the coming of Antichrist, being armed with divine signs and miracles, to engage with him in battle, and to be slain by him at Jerusalem, and to be taken up alive again into the clouds, after three days and a half.

And while the holy Enoch and Elijah were relating this, behold, there came another man in a miserable figure carrying the sign of the cross upon his shoulders. And when all saints saw him, they told him, who are you? For thy countenance is like a thief, and why do you carry a cross upon thy shoulders?

To which he answers, said, you say right, for I was a thief who committed all sorts of wickedness upon earth. And the Jews crucified me with Jesus, and I saw the supervising things which happened in the creation at the crucifixion of the Lord Jesus. (The Lost Books of the Bible, Nicodemus, Pg.82-88,1926).

And I believed him to be the Creator of all things and the Almighty King; and I prayed to him, saying, Lord, remember me when you come into your kingdom. He regarded my supplication and said, Verily I say unto you, thou shall be with me in paradise this day. (The Lost Books of the Bible, Nicodemus, Pg.82-88,1926).

And he gave me this sign of the cross saying, carry this, and go to paradise; and if the angel who is the guard of heaven will not admit you show him the sign of the cross, and say unto him: Jesus Christ who is now crucified has sent me here to you.

When I did this and told the angel who is the guard of paradise all these things, and he heard them, he presently opened the gates, introduced me, and placed me on the right-hand in paradise.

Saying, stay here a little time till Adam, the father of all humanity, shall enter in, with all his sons, who are holy and righteous servants of Jesus Christ, who was crucified. When they heard all this account from the thief, all the fathers said with one voice, Blessed be you, O Almighty God, the Father of everlasting goodness, and the Father of mercies, who has shown such favor to those who were sinners against him, and has brought them to the mercy of paradise, and has placed them amid the extensive and spiritual provisions, in spiritual and holy life.

Amen. (The Lost Books of the Bible, Nicodemus, Pg.82-88,1926).

CHAPTER 11
KEYS TO THE PLATES OF HELL

1. *Entrance to the confines of Hell.*

2. *Charon in his bark.*

3. *The Minotaur roared at the approach of condemned souls.*

4. *Souls agitated by the impure breath of evil spirits.*

5. *Cerberus devouring the souls of gourmands.*

6. *The Avaricious and prodigal condemned to carry burdens.*

7. *The envious and angry cast into the Styx.*

8. *Tower and wall of the evil city.*

9. *In this ditch are those who have sinned against their neighbors; Centaurs shoot arrows at them.*

10. *Harpies here torment those who have sinned against themselves.*

11. *Rain of fire for those who have sinned against God.*

12. *The soul of the tyrant Gerion was cast into the flames.*

13. *Debauches and corruptors of youth flogged by devils.*

14. *Poisonous gulf into which flatterers are plunged.*

15. *Lake of fire in the caldrons into which Simonaics are cast.*

16. *Sorcerers and diviners, their faces turned backward.*

17. *Bog of the boiling pitch for cheats, thieves, and deceivers.*
(The Lost Books of the Bible, Nicodemus, Pg.82-88,1926).

18. *Hypocrite crucified.*

19. *Treacherous advisers plunged into a flaming ditch.*

20. *For scandalous people, one holds his head in his hand.*

21. *Robbers and other criminals tormented by a centaur armed with serpents.*

22. *Alchemists and quacks are prey to leprosy.*

23. *Well of ice, for traitors and the ungrateful.*

24. *Pluto amid a glacier devouring the damned.*

25. *The holy city of Jerusalem.*
(The Lost Books of the Bible, Nicodemus, Pg.82-88,1926).

CHAPTER 12
REVELATION 20

Revelation is the most debated chapter in the Bible, not because it has anything tricky but because it touches on a subject of decided prejudice. Now is the time when Satan will be taken, bound, and put into the bottomless pit of the abyss, where his influence will not have any effect on the tribulation Saints who have lived through the seven years of tribulation. Can you see a life where Satan isn't around to tempt us? We think the 1000-year millennium will be a time of paradise. That nothing wrong will happen? We must enter the 1000-year millennium as believers. Most will live for a thousand years and procreate and have children. Yes, even the curse on the animals is lifted, and the wolves will lie down with the lamb and live in peace with each other.

But humanity is what it is. The children of those Saints will still have to be taught about Jesus; even though He will be with them constantly, many will not accept Him. Remember, the heart is evil, and unfortunately, that is the nature of man. Many of those children will be rebels, and with a tremendous population explosion during those one thousand years, there will probably be multitudes of people at the end, much like it is now. However, the unbelievers at that point will be as "the number of whom is as the sand of the sea."

In verses 1-3, The "bottomless pit" is the Abyss; the Greek word abusers are the abode of evil spirits (Rev.9:1-11; Luke 8:31). The "key" shows authority, and the "chain" describes imprisonment and binding. Before the millennial kingdom begins, "Satan" (Rev, 12:9) is "bound" in the Abyss.

The "seal" shows God's authority and guarantees that Satan will not be released until "a thousand years" have passed. During the Millennium (Latin:" one thousand years"), Satan will not be able to tempt or "deceive the nations."

Any temptation to sin during the Millennium must come from those born after the kingdom begins. It must be accepted that all of Satan's demons or fallen angels are also imprisoned at that time (Isa. 24:21-23).

Christ will reign on earth without opposition, and His kingdom will be characterized by righteousness, peace, and love (Isa. 2:3-4; 11:3-5; 35:1- 2; Dan. 7:14; Zech. 14:9). However, after the thousand years, Satan will be released for a short time.

Revelation 20:1: "And I saw an angel come down from heaven, having the key to the bottomless pit and a great chain in his hand."

This "angel" is not Jesus Himself but is a ministering spirit to whom Jesus has given authority. This angel comes from heaven near the throne of God. We can imagine from this that Jesus has turned the key to the bottomless pit over to this special angel and has given him power and authority for this job.

The _"great chain"_ in this angel's hand shows the power God has given him over the devil for this task, to keep him from deceiving the nations anymore until the thousand years have ended.

"Key of the bottomless pit": The place where demons are incarcerated pending their final sentencing to the lake of fire (Rev.9:1; 2 Peter 2:4).

Revelation 20:2: "And he laid hold on the dragon, that old serpent, which is the Devil, and Satan, and bound him a thousand years,"

"Laid hold": This includes not only Satan but the demons as well "Satan." Their imprisonment will significantly alter the world during the kingdom since their destructive influence in all areas of human thought and life will be removed.

"Dragon": Likening Satan to a dragon emphasizes his ferocity and cruelty.

Here, we see the devil spoken of as the dragon, which we read about in a previous scripture (Rev. 12:3).

We also see him identified as the serpent. He was the one who deceived Eve in the garden (Gen. 3:1; 2 Cor. 11:3; 1 Tim. 2:14).

The devil will not be here on the earth to harass the Christians until the millennial 1000-year reign of Jesus is over.

When he bound the devil for 1000- years, the angel put him in the abyss, not in the burning hell. This burning hell is reserved for his final punishment.

"A thousand years": This is the first of six references to the length of the millennial kingdom. There are three main interpretations of the duration and nature of this period:

1. Premillennialism this literal 1000-year period during which Jesus Christ, in fulfillment of numerous prophecies (2 Sam. 7:12-16; Psalm 2; Isa. 11:6-12; 24:23; Hosea 3:4-5; Joel 3:9-21; Amos 9:8-15; Micah 4:1-8; Zeph. 3:14-20; Zech. 14:1-11; Matt. 24:29- 31, 36:44), reigns on the earth.

    *   Using the same general principles of interpretation for both prophetic and non-prophetic passages lead most naturally to Premillennialism.

    *   Another strong argument supporting this view is that so many biblical prophecies have been accurately fulfilled, indicating that future prophecies will likewise be fulfilled plainly.

2. (Postmillennialism understands the reference to 1000 years as only symbolic of a golden age of righteousness and spiritual prosperity.

- It will be ushered in by the gospel's spread during the present church age and brought to completion when Christ returns.

- According to this interpretation, references to Christ's reign on earth primarily describe His spiritual reign in the hearts of believers in the church.

3. Amillennialism understands the 1000- years as simply symbolic of an extended period. This view interprets Old Testament prophecies of a Millennium as being fulfilled spiritually now in the church either on earth or in heaven or as references to the eternal state.

  - However, with the same literal, historical, and grammatical principle of interpretation to determine the usual sense of language, one is left with the inescapable conclusion that Christ will return and reign in a real kingdom on earth for 1000- years.

  - There is nothing in the text to render the conclusion that "a thousand years" is symbolic. Never is Scripture when "year" is used with a number is its meaning not literal (2 Peter 3:8).

Revelation 20:3: "And cast him into the bottomless pit, and shut him up, and set a seal upon him, that he should deceive the nations no more, till the thousand years should be fulfilled: and after that, he must be loosed a little season."

"The bottomless pit": All seven times that this appears in Revelation, it refers to where fallen angels and evil spirits are kept captive, waiting to be sent to the lake of fire, the final hell prepared for them (Matt. 25:41).

"Be loosed a little season": Satan will be released so God can make a permanent end of sin before establishing the new heaven and earth.

All who survive the Tribulation and enter the kingdom will be believers. However, despite that and the personal presence and rule of the Lord Jesus Christ, many of their descendants will refuse to believe in Him.

Satan will then gather those unbelievers for one final, ineffectual rebellion against God.

It will be quickly and positively crushed, followed by the Great White Throne Judgment and the establishment of the eternal state.

At the end of the 1000- years, Satan will once again be released to deceive the nations. He will find many unsaved descendants of those who lived through the millennium. There will be a considerable number, as we are told in verse eight, as they will be like the sand of the seashore or a vast, uncountable multitude.

Satan's deceitful way of getting those sinners to revolt against God is not revealed, but it will fit into God's plan when He destroys those rebels.

These rebels will come from the earth's four corners, also known as Gog and Magog.

- "Gog and Magog,

- "Mark of the Beast".

"Reigned": Tribulation believers and the redeemed from both the Old Testament and New Testament times will reign with Christ (1 Cor. 6:2; 2 Tim. 2:12) during the 1000-year kingdom. Many writers do not believe this thousand year is a precise time. They think that this is spiritual, and that Jesus bound the devil when He defeated him on the cross. If that were so, who is this terrible thing that has been nipping at our heels all the time that we have been working for God? The devil is real. Just as he brought trials and tribulation on Job with permission from God, Christians are allowed to go through tribulation here on this earth to make them strong. Believe me; the devil is not locked up now.

In the scripture above, we find that the martyrs and those who refuse to take the mark of the beast will reign with Christ right here on this earth. Christians, from all generations, will live here on this earth during the millennium and will rule and reign with the Lord Jesus. We will rule with Christ during those years, but we will not be equal as we will reign as His subordinates. Won't it be wonderful to reign with martyrs like Stephen?

We believe this 1000-year Millennial reign of Jesus Christ must be 1000- years. Humanity has worked six 1000-year days since Adam, which will be the one "1000"- year day of rest sabbath. God set this universe up on six days of work and one day of rest. The land was set to work for six years and one year of rest. Jesus hung on the cross for six hours to complete his work. Conforming to God's pattern will be a literal 1000- years of rest.

The thrones represent the administration of the messianic kingdom. Those whom John sees come to life are the Tribulation martyrs who refused to worship the beast. Christ will rule through three classes of kingdom administrators:

- Old Testament saints (Isaiah 26:19; Dan. 12:2), who will be resurrected now.

- The apostles and the church (Matt. 19:28-29); and

- Tribulation saints (Luke 19:12-27).

- Only believers will enter the Millennium at its beginning (John 3:3- 5).

God's promises to Abraham (Gen. 12:2-3) and David (2 Sam 7:16) will be fulfilled (Luke 1:31-33; Rom. 11:15, 29). After the Millennium, Christ will deliver the kingdom to God the Father and be appointed Ruler forever (1 Cor. 15:24-28).

The *"first resurrection"* is the resurrection included in verse 4. It has three principal phases:

- *The resurrection of Christ -the first fruits.* (1 Cor. 15:23; Rev. 1:5);

- *The resurrection of the church -the dead in Christ.* (1 Cor. 15:23; 1 Thess. 4:16); and

- *The resurrection of -Old Testament and Tribulation saints.* (Isa. 26:19; Dan. 12:2).

The *"rest of the dead" (unbelievers)* will be raised in the second resurrection, as explained (Rev. 20:12-13).

Revelation 20:4: "And I saw thrones, and they sat upon them, and judgment was given unto them: and [I saw] the souls of them that were beheaded for the witness of Jesus, and the word of God, and which had not worshipped the beast, neither his image, neither had received his mark upon their foreheads, nor in their hands, and they lived and reigned with Christ a thousand years."

The *"thrones"* represent the administration of the messianic kingdom.

- Those whom John sees come to life are the Tribulation martyrs who refused to worship the "beast."

- They will rule the earth "with Christ" for "a thousand years."

- Christ will rule through three classes of kingdom administrators:

1. Old Testament saints (Isa. 26:19; Dan. 12:2), who will be resurrected now.

2. The apostles and the church (Matt. 19:28-29).

3. Tribulation saints (compare Luke 19:12-27).

Only believers will enter the Millennium at its beginning (John 3:3, 5). God's promises to Abraham (Gen. 12:2-3) and David (2 Sam. 7:16) will be fulfilled (Luke 1:31-33; Rom. 11:15, 29).

After the Millennium, Christ will deliver the kingdom to God the

Father and be appointed Ruler forever (1 Cor. 15:24-28).

"The souls of them that were beheaded":

- These are tribulation martyrs (Rev. 6:9; 18:24; 19:2).

- The Greek word translated as "beheaded" became a general term for execution, not necessarily a particular method of punishment.

- His mark" (Rev. 13:16).

- Tribulation martyrs will be executed for refusing the mark of the beast ("Mark of the Beast").

The first resurrection is a resurrection to life (John 5:28-29), whereas the second is a resurrection to death. The second death is eternal punishment in the lake of fire (Rev.20: 14).

Revelation 20:5: *"But the rest of the dead lived not again until the thousand years were finished. This the first resurrection."*

The rapture of the church is the first resurrection. Those dead who did not accept the Lord as their Savior have not risen from the grave yet. They will be in the book of damnation. This 1000-year is just for the resurrected Christians.

"The rest of the dead": The bodies of unbelievers of all ages will not be resurrected until the Great White Throne Judgment (Rev.20:12-13).

"First resurrection": Scripture teaches two kinds of resurrections:

- *The "resurrection of life" – The Book of Life*

- *The "resurrection of judgment"- The Book of Damnation (John 5:29; Dan. 12:2; Acts 24:15).*

- *The first kind of resurrection is "the resurrection of the righteous" (Luke 14:14).*

- *The resurrection of "those who are Christ's at His coming" (1 Cor. 15:23).*

- *The "better resurrection" (Heb. 11:35).*

- *The redeemed of the church age (1 Thess. 4:13-18).*

- *The Old Testament (Dan. 12:2), and the Tribulation (verse 4).*

- *They will enter the kingdom in resurrection bodies and believers who survived the Tribulation. (The Book of Life).*

- *The second kind of resurrection, then, will be the resurrection of the unconverted, who will receive their final bodies suited for torment in hell. (The Book of Damnation).*

The first resurrection is the resurrection. It has three principal phases:

- *The resurrection of Christ -the first fruits. 1 Cor. 15:23; Rev. 1:5).*

- *The resurrection of the church -the dead in Christ. (1 Cor. 15:23; 1 Thess. 4:16).*

- *The resurrection of- Old Testament and Tribulation saints (Rev.20:4; Isaiah 26:19; Dan. 12:2).*

- *The rest of the dead- unbelievers, will be raised in the second resurrection, as described (Rev.20:12-13).*

- *The first resurrection is a resurrection to life- The Book of Life. (John 5:28-29).*

- *The second resurrection is a resurrection to death.*

- *The second death is eternal punishment in the lake of fire – The Book of Damnation. (Rev. 20:14)*

Revelation 20:6: "Blessed and holy is he that hath part in the first resurrection: on such the second death hath no power, but they shall be priests of God and Christ and shall reign with him a thousand years."

"Blessed":

- Those who die in the Lord (Rev. 14:13)

- Are blessed with the privilege of entering His kingdom (Rev. 1:3).

We Christians are blessed. You can easily see that the wicked dead have no part in this resurrection.

We believers in Christ the redeemed are not subject to death because we have life, which Jesus breathed into us when we were born again. We will never die.

This *second death* mentioned here is for the lost. (The Book of Damnation). Not only will the Christians reign on this earth with Jesus for 1000- years, but we will live for all eternity in heaven with Jesus because we have eaten of the Tree of Life, Jesus Christ our Lord.

"Second death": The first is only physical; the second is spiritual and eternal in the lake of fire, the final, eternal hell. (*The Book of Damnation, Rev. 14*). It could exist outside the created universe as we know it, outside of space and time, and is presently occupied with the damned. (Rev. 19:20 for the first two occupants).

This second death mentioned here is for the lost. Not only will the Christians reign on this earth with Jesus for 1000- years, but we will live for all eternity in heaven with Jesus because we have eaten of the Tree of Life, Jesus Christ our Lord.

What is the Millennium?

Christ's 1000-year reign upon David's throne fulfills God's promises to Abraham, Isaac, Israel, and David, but it's more than that; it is the final proof of the intractable nature of man's sinful heart.

Christ is present in Jerusalem, ruling the world, and the saints of all ages in resurrected bodies administer the kingdom righteously under His direction. All evil is prohibited and punished immediately.

Even Satan is locked away so that he cannot in any way influence humanity (Rev. 20:2).

Many believers who enter the Millennium in their natural bodies as survivors of the Tribulation (Matt. 25:34, Matt. 24) will begin to have children, who will also reproduce throughout the "thousand years."

Many of those descendants will remain unsaved and unregenerate and, therefore, be able to sin.

At the end of the Millennium, "Satan" will be released from prison to make one last attempt to defeat Christ. He will "deceive the nations" into rebellion against God.

The reference to *"Gog and Magog"* shows that this final battle will be like the invasion described in (Ezekiel 38).

The *"beloved city"* is the earthly Jerusalem, the headquarters of Christ's millennial kingdom (Isa. 60:1-22; Zech. 14:1-20). The rebels will be quickly destroyed by "fire … from God". Satan will then be "cast into the lake of fire," where his henchmen, the Beast, the Antichrist, and the False Prophet are (Rev. 20:10, 15; 19:20). Their torment will be eternal.

Revelation 20:7: "And when the thousand years are expired, Satan shall be loosed out of his prison,"

"Satan … loosed":

- He is loosed to bring unified leadership to the world of rebels born to the believers who entered the kingdom initially.

- He is loose to reveal the approval of Christ-rejecting sinners brought into judgment for the last time ever.

Satan and his demons will be imprisoned in the abyss for 1000-years while Christ rules with unopposed sovereignty. They are not permitted to interfere in the kingdom's affairs.

All those who initially went into the kingdom were, without a doubt, redeemed sinners who had turned to Christ in faith. The bad news is that they still will possess a sinful human nature. That sin nature is passed on to their children, grandchildren, and generations.

Thus, each generation born in the millennium will need salvation. Many will come to salvation, but amazingly, despite the most moral society the world will ever know, a significant number will love like sin and reject Him.

When Satan is loosed, he provides the leadership needed to bring the hidden sin and rebellion to the surface of those unrepentant sinners. It is an act of rebellion that will start when he is released.

Revelation 20:8: "And shall go out to deceive the nations which are in the four quarters of the earth, Gog and Magog, to gather them together to battle: the number of whom is as the sand of the sea."

This *"battle"* is very similar to the battle we read about in chapter 19 of Revelation. The only thing that makes this appear to be a different battle is that the one in chapter 19 happens in the valley of Megiddo. And this battle seems to be around the city of Jerusalem.

"Gog and Magog":

- The name was given to the army of rebels and its leader at the end of the Millennium.

- They were names of ancient enemies of the Lord.

- Magog was the grandson of Noah (Gen. 10:2)

- and the founder of a kingdom located north of the Black and Caspian Seas.

- Gog is the leader of a rebel army known jointly as Magog.

- The battle depicted (in verses 8-9) is like the one in Ezek. chapters 38 and 39).

- It is best to see this one as taking place at the end of the Millennium, not the Tribulation.

The use of Gog and Magog here and (in Ezekiel 38 and 39), has confused some readers,

- A thorough reading of the two passages reveals that the events are different.

- The one thing these events have in common is that the spirit of rebellion against God drives both national entities (Gog and Magog).

- In these two cases, God uses the same names because of the fraudulently satanic spirit that motivates them both ("Gog and Magog").

Ezek. 38:2: "Son of man, set thy face against Gog, the land of Magog, the chief prince of Meshech and Tubal, and prophesy against him,"

"Meshech and Tubal": Chief Prince,

- Two peoples were recognized in ancient Assyrian monuments: Mushki (Mushku) and Tubal (Tabal).

- Both were in Asia Minor, the area of Magog, modern-day Turkey.

- Summing up, a chief prince, who is the enemy of God's people, will lead a coalition of nations against Jerusalem.

- Ezekiel details the enemy force and its destruction in the rest of chapters 38 and 39.

Ezekiel 38:3 "And say, thus saith the Lord GOD; Behold, I am against thee, O Gog, *the chief prince of Meshech and Tubal:."*

In Ezekiel 38 and 39, we read detailed information about a similar battle. I believe "Gog and Magog" are modern Russia is Gog. When you read this in Ezekiel, you will see Iran (Persia), Libya, Ethiopia, and Turkey. All of these are already having problems with Israel.

Look at these two scriptures:

Ezekiel 39:12: "And seven months shall the house of Israel be burying of them, that they may cleanse the land."

Ezekiel 39:9: "And they that dwell in the cities of Israel shall go forth, and shall set on fire and burn the weapons, both the shields and the bucklers, the bows and the arrows, and the hand staves, and the spears, and they shall burn them with fire seven years:"

When you look at the following scripture, you see a problem with the seven months and years of Ezekiel, which doesn't fit the timing here. As in 20:9, that is pretty much the end of everything. So, you decide if this is two battles or one. One is at the end just before the start of the Tribulation or into the beginning of the Tribulation, and the second is to end the world as we know it at the end of the Millennium.

They will muster their forces from one corner of the globe to another and march on Jerusalem, where they will "surround the camp of the saints and the beloved city." But there will be no battle. No call to arms. No defensive strategy or late-night negotiations, propaganda campaign, or deploying of gigantic nuclear weapons.

The four quarters of the earth refer to the entire globe. Gog is used as a title for an enemy of God's people, not a particular person. Magog seems to be the term used here to describe the area where the sinful rebels of all the nations come from that gathering for the last war in human history.

The number of these rebels will be like the sand of the seashore, a figure of speech used in the bible to define a vast and unaccountable multitude. Consider how when Joseph sent for his father and family, 70 people came to Egypt. A little over 400 years later, there were millions whom God led out of Egypt. More people will be left than 70 going into the millennium, and there will be 250% more time for procreation. There will probably be many billions of people at that time, so Satan could have a huge gathering that will join for that final battle. "The number of whom is as the sand of the sea."

Revelation 20:9: "And they went up on the breadth of the earth, and compassed the camp of the saints about, and the beloved city: and fire came down from God out of heaven and devoured them."

These enemies of God here come against Jesus and the saints. They surround the saints. The *"beloved city"* mentioned here is Jerusalem. When the devil thinks he has won, fire comes down from heaven from God and devours them.

"Fire":

- They are often associated in Scripture with the divine judgment of wicked men (Gen 19:24; 2 Kings 1:10, 12, 14; Luke 9:54; 17:29).

Again, like in the battle of Armageddon before the millennium started, this battle will be an execution. As the rebel forces moved into attack, they were swiftly and exterminated.

They will be physically killed, and their souls will go into the realm of punishment, awaiting final sentencing to the eternal hell that will shortly take place.

Revelation 20:10: "And the devil that deceived them was cast into the lake of fire and brimstone, where the beast and the false prophet are, and shall be tormented day and night forever."

"Deceived": Just as his demons will entice the world's armies into the *Battle of Armageddon,* Satan will draw them into a suicidal assault against Christ and those with Him (Rev.16:13-14).

"Lake of fire and brimstone" (Rev. 19:20).

The beast and false prophet have been waiting for Satan in the lake of fire and brimstone for the last one thousand years. Now, their deceiver joins them.

"Tormented day and night" (Rev. 14:11). Continuous, unrelieved torment will be the final state of Satan, fallen angels, and unredeemed men. There will not be a moment's peace for them all the rest of

eternity:

- These verses describe the final judgment of all the unbelievers of all ages (Matt. 10:15; 11:22, 24; 12:36, 41-42; Luke 10:14; John 12:48; Acts 17:31, 24:25; Rom. 2:5, 16; Heb. 9:27; 2 Peter 2:9; 3:7; Jude 6).

- Our Lord called this event the "resurrection of judgment" (John 5:29).

- This judgment occurs in the indescribable void between the end of the present universe (verse 11) and the creation of the new heaven and earth (21:1).

Revelation 20:11: "And I saw a great white throne, and him that sat on it, from whose face the earth and the heaven fled away; and there was found no place for them."

"Great white throne":

- Nearly fifty times in Revelation, there is the mention of a throne.

- It is a judgment throne, elevated, pure, and holy ("Great White Throne – Judgment Seat").

- God sits on it as judge (Rev. 4:2-3, 9; 5:1, 7, 13; 6:16; 7:10, 15), in the person of the Lord Jesus Christ (Rev. 21:5-6; John 5:22-29; Acts 17:31).

The judgment day.

- Now, John describes the terrifying scene set before him.

- He sees the Judge Seated on His throne of Judgment and all of the accused standing before Him.

- The verdicts handed down from this throne will be equitable, righteous, and just.

"The earth and the heaven fled away":

- John saw the contaminated universe go out of existence.

- Peter described this moment (2 Peter 3:10-13).

- The universe is "uncreated," going into non-existence (Matt. 24:35; "Destruction of the Earth by God").

We also remember (Ecclesiastes 12:14), which promises, "God shall bring every work into judgment, with every secret thing, whether it be good or evil." As well as (Romans 2:5-6), Paul speaks of the day of God's wrath "when his righteous judgment will be revealed.

God will give to each person according to what he has done". It is a fearful thing even to imagine standing before God "from whose face the earth and the heaven fled away" and have nothing but your wicked works to show for the time on earth the Almighty had given you.

On that day, the words of Paul, the apostle will come true: "Now we know that whatever the law says, it says to those who are under the law, so that every mouth may be silenced and the whole world held accountable to God" (Rom. 3:19). The final word, of course, will be God's.

This vision follows those of the Second Coming: **RAPTURE**

- ("Glorious Appearance – Second Coming of Christ"), and those of the Millennium, immediately preceding the new heaven and new earth ("New Heaven and the New Earth").

- The use of the earth is over.

- The earth, heaven, and everything in them are under the control of God, and if He tells them to go, they will have to.

- It is an excellent, incredible statement describing the universe's un-creation.

- The earth was reshaped by the tribulation judgments, restored during the millennial kingdom, and now God will create a new heaven and world as it says (2 Peter 3).

2 Peter 3:13: "Nevertheless we, according to his promise, look

for new heavens and a new earth, wherein dwelleth righteousness."

The "dead" are *the unbelieving dead of all the ages,* the "rest of the dead" mentioned (Rev.20:5).

- They are *"judged"* from two sets of books *("Book of Life – All Books, The Book of Damnation").*

- The *"books"* have the record of every unsaved person's life.

- Each *unsaved person is judged* following their "works" (Rom. 2:6, 16),

- Which clearly shows that each one is *a guilty sinner* (Rom. 3:9- 19),

- *Deserving of eternal death* (Rom. 3:23; 6:23)

- *The "book of life"* has the name of every person who has received eternal life through faith alone (John 20:31; 1 John 5:11-13).

- *These unsaved people* are shown that they did not take advantage of the offer of eternal life through faith (Rom. 9:32; 10:3). "

- *Death and hell"* (Hades) are the temporary holding places of unsaved men's bodies and souls, respectively (Luke 16:19-31).

Revelation 20:12: "And I saw the dead, small and great, stand before God, and the books were opened: and another book was opened, which is [the book] of life: and the dead were judged out of those things which were written in the books, according to their works."

"Stand before God":

- In a judicial sense, as guilty, condemned prisoners before the bar of divine justice.

- There are no living sinners left in the destroyed universe since all sinners were killed and all believers glorified.

The *"dead"* are:

- Those who are spiritually dead because they reject Christ.

- They will stand in their resurrected state before Jesus to be judged by Him.

"Books":

- These books record every thought, word, and deed of sinful men, all recorded by divine omniscience (Dan. 7:9-10).

- They will provide the evidence for eternal condemnation (Rev.18:6-7).

- These statements at once call our attention back to the words of the Lord Jesus: "What you have said in the dark will be heard in the daylight, and what you have whispered in the ear in the inner rooms will be proclaimed from the roofs" (Luke 12:3).

- And "There is nothing hidden that will not be disclosed, and nothing concealed that will not be known or brought out into the open" (Luke 8:17).

Remember that the Christian dead:

- *They had already won their victory.*

- Jesus judged those at the Bema Seat ("Bema Seat – A Judgment Seat for Christians").

- Now is this final fearful scene, where these include all *unbelievers who have ever lived.*

- It is *the resurrection of judgment,* and they stand before Christ now at *the White Throne Judgment ("Great White Throne Judgment Seat").*

- The scope of *the scene is chilling.*

- *The great mass of these unbelievers* before God's throne includes everyone from presidents and kings to ").

- Some books contain a *person's every thought, word, and deed.*

- *Nothing will be hidden.*

- Think about the fact that God knows *the secrets of one's heart.*

- *Those who didn't accept Jesus* must stand or fall on their deeds.

- Of course, they will all fall if they *don't accept Him* because all have sinned and come short of the glory of God.

- *The blood of Jesus has done away with the Christian's sins.*

- God has kept perfect, comprehensive, and accurate records of every person's life (deeds), which will be measured against God's perfect and holy standard.

- Those who didn't accept Jesus must stand or fall on their deeds.

- Of course, they will all fall if they don't accept Him because scripture tells us that "all have sinned and come short of the glory of God."

"Book of life":

- It contains the names of all the redeemed (Dan. 12:1; see notes on 3:5).

The Book of Life is the Lamb's Book of Life:

- Where the names of all believers who have accepted, believed, and followed Christ are written.

- The blood of Jesus has taken the Christian's sins away.

- Those Christians all have their names written in the Lamb's book of life and will not taste the second death.

"Judged ... according to their deeds":

- Their thoughts (Luke 8:17; Rom. 2:16),

- Words (Matt. 12:37),

- Actions (Matt. 16:27) will be compared to God's perfect, holy standard (Matt. 5:48; 1 Peter 1:15-16) and will be found wanting (Rom. 3:23).

- It also implies that hell has degrees of punishment (Matt. 10:14-15; 11:22; Mark 12:38-40; Luke 12:47-48: Heb. 10:29).

Revelation 20:13: "And the sea gave up the dead which was in it, and death and hell delivered up the dead which were in them: and they were judged every man according to their works."

"Death and hell" (1:18). Both terms describe the state of death:

- The unrighteous dead will appear at the Great White Throne Judgment; none will escape.

- All the places that have held the bodies of the unrighteous dead will yield up new bodies suited for hell.

- Those who are lost wait in torment in a place of punishment until judgment day.

- The terrible thing is that they are aware that they will be thrown into the lake of fire on judgment day.

- These are all the unbelievers though out the ages who have died.

- Christ will raise them for judgment called the second resurrection.

Before the sea was uncreated and disappeared out of existence, it gave up the dead that was in it. The sea may be mentioned as it is seemingly the most challenging place from which dead bodies could be resurrected. But God will summon new bodies for all who perished in the sea throughout history.

Death symbolizes all the places on land from which God will resurrect new bodies for the unrighteous, unrepentant dead.

As the next scene in this courtroom drama unfolds:

- The lost will be summoned to appear before the judge.

- Since their deaths, their souls have been tormented in a place of punishment; now, the time has finally come for them to be judged and sentenced.

Revelation 20:14: "And death and hell were cast into the lake of fire. It is the second death."

The *"second death"* is:

- Eternal punishment in the lake of fire, experienced only by the unsaved.

- Once this final judgment occurs, there is no further need for either death or hell (Hades; 1:18; 6:8, Isaiah 25:8; 1 Cor. 15:26-55).

- An eternal separation is now between those who have life and those who have "death" (Dan. 12:2; John 5:29).

- It does not mean these places are thrown into the lake. It means the inhabitants of these places.

Revelation 20:15: "And whosoever was not found written in the book of life was cast into the lake of fire."

The scriptures never refer to death as the mere cessation of life but instead, as the unnatural separation of something from that to which it belongs.

- Therefore, a body without the spirit suffers physical death (Gen. 35:18).

- The expression *"second death"* defines the separation of a man from God.

- Human consciousness is conveyed in the biblical description of the second death, suggesting that the beast and the False Prophet will remain alive for a thousand years after being cast into the lake of fire (19:20; 20:10).

- When saved, a person has passed from death to life and can be assured he will never come into condemnation (John 5:24; see Gen. 2:17; Mark 9:43).

The final hell:

- Described as the lake of fire.

- It already exists but is occupied until the beast and the false prophet are cast into it. They don't arrive there until the end of the Tribulation.

- Those who die in their sins in this world will die a second death in eternity.

- They will be sentenced to the lake of fire forever at the great White Throne Judgment ("Judgment on Mankind is Coming").

Whether this *fire is symbolic:*

- The reality it represents will be even more horrifying and painful.

- The bible also defines hell as a place of total darkness, which not only separates the unbelievers from the light but from each other as well.

What is written in these last two verses should drive us to continue to spread the gospel if there is breath in our bodies. I cannot bear to think of anyone I know going to this terrible place of torment.

And that's it. In a ball of celestial flame, the rebellion is over. There will be no repeat of the Tribulation's plagues nor the Great

Tribulation's judgments. Once and for all, human rebellion will have been wiped out of existence.

And once and for all, it will be crystal clear to a watching universe that the death and resurrection of Jesus Christ are essential for making the unrighteous human heart into a receptacle of God's holiness.

The Millennium will prove that even the best conditions, a thousand years of peace, prosperity, safety, long life, health, and abundance, cannot change the wickedness of the unredeemed human heart. Only the Lord Jesus Christ can do that!

Excellent is the Word of God!

- It probably is not humanly possible to meditate on these astonishing truths for extended periods.

- Who can long ponder the lake of fire, an eternal place of torment, possibly billions of unredeemed souls,

- A divine Person "from whose face the earth and the heaven fled away," or fear some books of judgment that seal the fate of the unsaved?

- And yet our Lord tells us of these remarkable events.

- Why? To give us every opportunity to escape the terrible judgment that is to come.

- Remember, "no believer in Christ" will stand before God on the great white throne.

- That terrible spot is reserved only for those who have rejected Christ as Savior, who have decided to crown themselves king, and who have refused to accept Jesus Christ as their faithful Lord.

- Do not make that terrible mistake!

- Instead, place your faith in the Lord Jesus and ask Him to forgive your sins; then, you will be ready "to stand before the Son of Man" at the judgment seat of Christ (Luke 21:36).

- One thing is sure: You will stand in one place or the other.

- Hell, or heaven.

- Make sure it's the latter.

- And don't think that you can choose not to believe there is such a thing as heaven or hell, as it makes no difference.

- Everyone will be judged and assigned to one place or the other.

- It is the same on earth; ignorance is no excuse for the law!

Getting your name written in the Lamb's Book of Life is easy.

Acts 2:38: "Then Peter said unto them, Repent, and be baptized every one of you in the name of Jesus Christ for the remission of sins, and ye shall receive the gift of the Holy Ghost."

"Repent":

- It refers to a change of mind and purpose that turns an individual from sin to God (1 Thess. 1:9).

- Such change involves more than fearing the consequences of God's judgment.

- Genuine repentance knows that the evil of sin must be forsaken, and the person and work of Christ totally and singularly embraced.

- Peter exhorted his hearers to repent, otherwise they would not experience true conversion (Matt. 3:2; Acts 3:19; 5:31; 8:22; 11:18; 17:30; 20:21; 26:20; Matt. 4:17)

"Be baptized":

- This Greek word means "be dipped or immersed" in water.

- Peter was obeying Christ's command from Matt. 28:19 and urging the people who repented and turned to the Lord Christ for salvation to show, through the waters of baptism, with His death, burial, and resurrection (Acts 19:5; Rom. 6:3-4; 1 Cor. 12:13; Gal. 3:27; see notes on Matt. 3:2).

- It was the first time the apostles publicly urged people to obey that ceremony.

- Before this, many Jews had experienced the baptism of John the Baptist (Matt. 3:1-3) and were also familiar with the baptism of Gentile converts to Judaism (proselytes).

"In the name of Jesus Christ"

- It was a crucial but costly identification for the new believer to accept.

"For the remission of sins":

- It might better be translated as "because of the forgiveness of sins." Baptism does not produce forgiveness and cleansing from sin. (1 Pet. 3:20-21).

- The reality of forgiveness precedes the rite of baptism (verse 41).

- Genuine repentance brings from God the forgiveness of sins (Eph. 1:7)

- Because of that, the new believer was to be baptized.

Baptism:

- However, it was to be the ever-present act of obedience so that it became synonymous with salvation.

- Thus, to say one was baptized for forgiveness was the same as saying one was saved,

- "One Baptism" (Eph. 4:5).

- Every believer fully forgives sins (Matt. 26:28; Luke 24:47; Eph. 1:7; Col. 2:13; 1 John 2:12).

Here, as throughout Scripture, one aspect of conversion is commonly used to stand for all aspects:

- Believing and calling, as well as repenting.

- Synecdoche is the grammatical name for allowing part of something to be the whole.

- Repentance is something every person must do (17:30).

- For several reasons, "be baptized" should not be joined with "for the remission of sins" to teach baptismal regeneration.

- First, the context of this passage proves that only repentance relates to the removal of sin at salvation: "Whosoever shall call ... shall be saved" (verse 21).

Peter's following recorded sermon states only.

- *"Repent* ... that your sins may be blotted out" (3:19).

- Second, throughout Acts, men prove their faith and salvation before baptism (10:43-47).

- Third, the soteriological passages throughout the New Testament do not include water baptism in the salvation experience – (John 3:16; Acts 16:31; Romans 4:10; Eph. 2:1-10; 1 Pet. 1:18-19).

Thus, this verse more clearly reads:

- *"Repent for the remission of sins,* and you will receive the gift, which is the Holy Spirit, and let each of you be baptized in the name of Christ."

- Though water baptism does not save or wash away our sins, it is a command that needs to be obeyed speedily after conversion.

- Jesus commanded it (Matt. 28:19-20), as does Peter.

- It is the consistent pattern throughout Acts (16:31-34; 18:8).

These men Peter was speaking to here were the house of Israel. They had rejected Jesus as their Messiah. They must repent of rejecting Jesus as the substitute for their sin. The one they had denied is the very one they are to be baptized in the name of Jesus. These are all Jews here.

They must repent of rejecting Jesus. They had the law; the Gentiles did not have the rule to follow.

"The gift of the Holy Ghost": (1:5, 8).

- Notice the gift of the Holy Ghost would come after they had repented and been baptized.

- Those who want to be saved must repent of their sin and believe in Jesus Christ's name.

- Just as Abraham was justified as if he had never sinned, they will be justified by faith in Jesus Christ.

- We read earlier how God will save all who call on His name.

Romans 10:9-10 "That if thou shalt confess with thy mouth the Lord Jesus, and shalt believe in thine heart that God hath raised him from the dead, thou shalt be saved." "For with the heart, man believeth unto righteousness; and with the mouth, confession is made unto salvation."

You see, Jesus should be our Lord as well as our Savior. If you genuinely believe, you will repent and be baptized. If your name is not written in the book of life, do not delay; do it today.

CHAPTER 13
REVELATION 17

Revelation chapter 17 returns and fills in some of what happened during the Tribulation. Chapter 16 is when the Great Tribulation is finished.

Chapter 17 details when Babylon the Harlot or the Religious Babylon is Destroyed ("Babylon the Harlot").

Archaeologists tell us that Babylon is the cradle of civilization. Located on the Euphrates River's shores, this city's ruins have revealed some of the most ancient documents of past generations.

This city was begun by Nimrod, who was a rebel before the Lord authored some of the greatest evils ever to fall on humankind. Two of these evils will be destroyed during the Tribulation period. Revelation seventeen is the destruction of religious Babylon that occurs about the center of the seven years after the Antichrist declares himself to be God and no longer needs the One World Order.

In chapter eighteen, we will read about the destruction of the commercial, political Babylon, which took place at the end of the Great Tribulation. In ancient days, Satan seemed to make Babylon the capital of this evil operation. From this headquarters was started false religion, humanity's attempt for self-government in defiance of God's will, and city dwellings for commercial and social purposes contrary to God's command to "be fruitful and increase in number and fill the earth" (Gen. 1:28).

These great evils, which have damned the souls of millions by substituting counterfeit solutions to natural human problems that would ordinarily lead a person to God, will all be destroyed at the end of the Tribulation period. Chapter 17 describes the coming judgment of God on the religious system that has enslaved humanity in superstitious darkness for centuries.

The woman is a great city: "The woman you saw is the great city that rules over the kings of the earth" (Rev. 17:18). Many have taken this to mean that the woman is the capital city of Antichrist's kingdom, but this cannot be, for Antichrist himself rules over the kings of the earth.

If the woman is not the Antichrist, what other possible explanation can we have for such unanimous world dominance? The only answer is the one system before which all kings, dictators, and nations have been forced to bow down throughout history, that is, the Babylonian religion of idolatry. One cannot go anywhere without being confronted with some semblance of idolatry.

No system in the world's history has enslaved more people than this awful religion. It should not take us by surprise that this prostitute woman, the religious system, is referred to as a city. When used symbolically, a woman is always intended to signify a spiritual or religious movement throughout the Scripture. If a good woman, it is "Jehovah's wife" or "the bride of Christ." If an evil woman, such as "a prostitute," it represents the corrupt religious system of idolatry.

Since the woman who rides the beast gets her authority from the beast, the Holy Spirit uses this description to show how religious Babylon and governmental Babylon are so intertwined they are presented together. However, they are destroyed at different times.

The prostitute's religious Babylon is destroyed by the "beast and the kings of the earth," who "hate the prostitute" and kill her.

It clears the way for the Antichrist to fulfill the lifetime dream of Satan to get people to worship him. She is destroyed in the middle of the Tribulation; Babylon, the governmental system, will be destroyed at the end, when commercial, political Babylon is destroyed (Rev. 18). With "Mystery Babylon, the mother of Prostitutes" out of the way, "all inhabitants of the earth will worship the beast, all whose names have not been written in the book of life belonging to the

Lamb that was slain from the creation of the world" (Rev. 13:8).

The Vision of the Woman

Ten details describe this woman:

- The great prostitute

- Who sits on many waters?

- With her, the kings of the earth committed adultery.

- The inhabitants of the world were intoxicated with the wine of her adulteries.

- A woman sitting on a scarlet beast.

- Dressed in purple and scarlet.

- Glittering with gold, precious stones, and pearls.

- She held a golden cup in her hand, filled with abominable things and the filth of her adulteries.

- On her forehead: Mystery Babylon the Great, the mother of Prostitutes and the Abomination of the Earth.

- Drunk with the blood of the saints, the blood of those who bore testimony to Jesus.

Even before we come to the angel's interpretation of this vision, we are not dealing with a mere human being, for no one woman can commit fornication with the kings of the earth, nor can a woman be "drunk with the blood of the saints, the blood of those who bore testimony to Jesus."

Revelation seventeen and eighteen the judgment of God on a system, empire, or city called Babylon the Great. It has a more detailed description of the seventh vial (16:17).

The "great whore" is named "BABYLON THE GREAT." Her "judgment" and the "waters" represent the various peoples and nations of the earth.

She "sits upon" them because she has worldwide influence. Her harlotry and "fornication" refer either to physical immorality or spiritual adultery.

Idolatry and religious apostasy

(Isa. 1:21; 23:16-17; Jer. 2:20-37; 13:27; Ezek. 16:15-43; Hosea 2:5; Nahum 3:4). The "kings" and "inhabitants of the earth" have opened their arms to her influence.

The "beast" is the first Beast of Revelation thirteen, the Antichrist and his empire.

Her sitting upon the Beast stands for the intimate association between the Antichrist and the harlot, an association of support, influence, or control.

Revelation 17:1 "And there came one of the seven angels which had the seven vials, and talked with me, saying unto me, come hither; I will show unto thee the judgment of the great whore that sits upon many waters:"

"Seven angels": The reference to these angels' links chapters 17 and 18 with the vial (bowl) and judgments (chapter 16), which extend to the second coming of Christ (see note on 16:17). Chapters 17 and 18 focus on one aspect of those vial judgments, the judgment of Babylon. The decisions already described are identified as targeting the final world system.

"Great whore" (Revelation 14:8).

- Prostitution often symbolizes idolatry or religious apostasy (Jer. 3:6-9; Ezek. 16:3; 20:30; Hosea 4:15; 5:3; 6:10; 9:1). Nineveh (Nahum 3:1, 4),

- Tyre (Isa. 23:17) and even Jerusalem (Isa. 1:21) are also depicted as harlot cities.

"Sits on many waters": This picture emphasizes the sovereign power of the harlot. The image of a ruler seated on a throne, ruling

the waters, symbolizes the nations of the world.

The "whore" here is not a literal woman. In Hosea, his wife, who was a whore, was speaking of Israel. Here, this "whore" is speaking of the idolatrous church. This statement "sits upon many waters" tells of large groups of people. This is not the true church. This is the apostate church. God calls it the harlot church, the church that is not faithful to God, the worldly church.

This church, while claiming to be Christian, finds many reasons to conform to the beast and the evil world system. It will be the one world religion that will appear after the church (Christians) has been raptured ("One World Religion").

However, without question, it is the part of the church that has compromised with the world and is no longer a chaste virgin in the sight of God. I genuinely believe that many churches fall into this category today. Worldliness has crept into our churches. The sad thing is that if she would repent, God would take her back, but she would not regret it.

The Bride of Christ is called a city, the part of the church that has not compromised. The other opposite side of that is the harlot. It is also called a city but is evil because of compromise. This is not only the apostate church in Rome but the apostate in many other churches. Again, the waters tell us this apostate church is throughout the masses.

Revelation 17:2 "With whom the kings of the earth have committed fornication, and the inhabitants of the earth have been made drunk with the wine of her fornication."

"*Kings* … have committed fornication": The harlot will ally herself with the world's political leaders. Fornication here does not refer to sexual sin but to idolatry. All the world rulers will be absorbed into the empire of Satan's false Christ.

"*Wine of her fornication*": The harlot's influence will extend beyond the world's rulers to the rest of humanity (verse 15; 13:8,

13:14).

The imagery does not describe actual wine and sexual sin but pictures the world's people being swept up into the intoxication and sin of a false system of religion. We see here that this universal apostasy, unfaithfulness to God, does not affect just one class of people. This unfaithfulness is from the rich and powerful kings to the very poor.

In the same way, a drunken person naturally has no earthly idea what he is doing, and this apostate group is so carried away with the world that they, too, do not realize the terribleness of what they are doing. God will judge this idolatrous church. Judgment begins at the house of God.

Revelation 17:3: "So he carried me away in the spirit into the wilderness: and I saw a woman sit upon a scarlet-colored beast, full of names of blasphemy, having seven heads and ten horns."

"In the spirit": Revelation 1:10, 4:2; 21:10). The Holy Spirit transports John into the wilderness, a deserted, lonely, and desolate wasteland, perhaps to give him a better understanding of the vision.

"A woman": The harlot, Babylon.

"Scarlet colored beast": The Antichrist (compare 13:14, 14:9; 16:10), who for a time will support and use the false religious system to effect world unity. Then, he will assume political control (verse 16). Scarlet is the color of luxury, splendor, and royalty.

"Full of names of blasphemy": Because of his self-deification (Revelation 13:1; Dan. 7:25; 11:36; 2 Thess. 2:4).

"Having seven heads and ten horns": This pictures the extent of Antichrist's political alliances (Revelation 17: 9-12; 13:1).

"wilderness" here, I believe, means the world. This "scarlet colored beast" shows evil world power.

Since this woman sits upon this beast, her power comes from this evil beast as it supports her. It appears this woman has decided to trust the strengths of this world over God's power.

Seven: denotes spiritually complete, ten world governments, and horns of power. You can easily see the woman on top of this thing; she guides it but receives support from the beast. The word "scarlet" can be very good or very evil. In this case, it is fierce.

This tremendous evil blasphemy that this woman (church) has committed is spiritual adultery, the watering down or changing of the Word of God.

The elegant clothing and jewelry of the "woman" show her wealth and attractiveness, but her activities are filthy and abominable to God. Her mystery name is *BABYLON THE GREAT".* Much of the world's idolatry can be traced back to historical Babylon (Gen. 11:1-9), including the motherchild cult of Semiramis-Tammuz (Jer. 44:16-19; Ezek. 8:9, 14).

Idols which entered other cultures as Ashtaroth-Baal, Aphrodite-Eros, Venus-Cupid, and even Madonna-Child. As the fountainhead of idolatry, Babylon the harlot is the *MOTHER OF HARLOTS AND ABOMINATION OF THE EARTH.* The harlot has killed many of God's "saints" and Christian "martyrs" throughout the ages and will do so again during the Tribulation period. Admiration" (Greek thauma) here means "amazement" (Revelation 13:3; 17:6).

Revelation 17:4 "And the woman was arrayed in purple and scarlet color, and decked with gold and precious stones and pearls, having a golden cup in her hand full of abominations and filthiness of her fornication:"

"Purple and scarlet": Royalty, nobility, and wealth colors. The woman is portrayed as a prostitute who has plied her trade successfully and becomes incredibly wealthy.

"Decked" Prostitutes often dress in fine clothes and precious jewels to allure their victims (Prov. 7:10). The religious harlot Babylon is no different, adorning herself to lure the nations into her

grasp.

"A golden cup": Still more evidence of the harlot's great wealth (Jer. 51:7), but the filthiness of her immorality defiles the pure gold. Just as a prostitute might first get her victim drunk, the harlot system deceives the nation into committing spiritual fornication with her.

"Fornication" here spoken of, I genuinely believe, is spiritual adultery or compromise with the world.

God will tolerate almost anything except the worship of someone else or something else. I genuinely believe this has to do with the watering down of Jesus (Who He is).

Ancient Babylon is a type or prefigure of this future Babylon. The harlot will do what Babylon did in the past:

• Oppress God's people, and

• Propagate a false religious system.

Semiramis, also known as Ishtar and Isis, who was both Nimrod's wife and mother, was worshiped as the "mother of god" and a "fertility goddess" because she had to be extremely fertile to give birth to all the pagan incarnate gods that represented Nimrod. Cush begat Nimrod: he began to be a mighty one in the earth. The color scheme of this one world religion (Rev. 17:4) is most revealing: "The woman was dressed in purple and scarlet." If you are familiar with pictures of the Vatican Council published in national magazines, you will have seen that the bishops and cardinals wore purple and scarlet robes.

You will also see that the pope and other church leaders are "glittering with gold, precious stones and pearls." They hold "a golden cup in their hand, filled with abominable things and the filthiness of their adulteries." These abominable things and adulteries are the idolatry and worship of gods other than Jesus Christ. In Rome, all manner of idols in the very headquarters of the Roman Church. More costly surroundings can scarcely be found than in the Vatican.

The Catholic Church is many times decorated this way, but I believe this includes all the apostate churches, Protestant and Catholic. Perhaps this is people sitting on a church pew but not being the bride of Christ. There are some in all churches, but most assuredly, the church in Rome. You can see great masses of gold, silver, and jewels.

Usually, when a church building is decked out like this, it is in an area where there is abject poverty.

"Purple" shows this was in the church because purple means godliness. It was a false godliness.

"Golden cup" also shows this is inside the church because gold symbolically means the purity of God. We know this "cup" belonged to God. It just means that the world's sins have been brought into the church.

"Fornication" here spoken of, I genuinely believe, is spiritual adultery or compromise with the world. God will tolerate almost anything except the worship of someone or something else. I genuinely believe this has to do with the watering down of Jesus.

Revelation 17:5: "And upon her forehead was a name written, *MYSTERY, BABYLON THE GREAT, THE MOTHER OF HARLOTS AND ABOMINATIONS OF THE EARTH.*"

"Forehead": It was customary for Roman prostitutes to wear a headband with their name on it (Jer. 3:3), parading their wretchedness for all to see. The harlot's forehead is embellished with a 3-fold title descriptive of the world's final false religious system.

"Mystery": A New Testament mystery is truth once hidden, but in the New Testament revealed (Matt. 13:11; Eph. 3:4-5). Spiritual Babylon's identity is yet to be announced. Thus, the precise details of how it will manifest in the world are unknown.

"BABYLON THE GREAT": This Babylon is distinct from the historical, geographical city of Babylon, which still existed in John's time. The details of John's vision cannot be applied to any historical town.

MOTHER OF HARLOTS": All false religion stems ultimately from Babel, or Babylon (Gen. 11;14:8). Just as God marked the 144,000 with the name of the Father, and just as the bride of Christ is marked with the name of Christ, we see here this group marked on the forehead. This name alone makes you know how evil and worldly this church is.

Though nominally Christian, this worldly part of the church is yet more faithful to the world than to God. Notice here that the church pretends to be Christian and does not do more to cause harm than those worldly people who claim to be lost. The worldly church always persecutes the faithful church.

The evil in the church is an abomination to God. It is a mystery how this could happen in the church. As the fountainhead of idolatry, Babylon the harlot is the _MOTHER OF HARLOTS AND ABOMINATIONS OF THE EARTH;_ the harlot has killed many of God's saints and Christian martyrs throughout the ages and will do so again during the Tribulation period.

Revelation "17:6 And I saw the woman drunken with the blood of the saints, and with the blood of the martyrs of Jesus: and when I saw her, I wondered with great admiration."

The Blood of the Saints … martyrs of Jesus": Some see the first group as Old Testament saints and the second as New Testament saints, an unimportant distinction since this picture the "witnesses," or martyrs, of the Tribulation. John's point is that the harlot is a murderer. The false religion has killed millions of believers over the centuries, and the final wrong system will be far more deadly than any that preceded it.

The faithless part of the church is guilty of the blood of the saints. In _Matthew 12:20,_ we read that Jesus says, "He that is not with me is against me." This watered-down church is causing significant problems for those who are sold out to God. We do know that Rome had a great deal to do with the death of the martyrs and even had a hand in crucifying Jesus.

Of course, the Jewish church of that day had even more to do with the crucifixion of Jesus. However, the most blame for His death must be placed on each of us. Sin put Jesus on the cross. He went to the cross to crucify sin. His sacrifice stopped us from being a servant to sin.

The wonder is that with the Bible as their guide, how could these people get so far away from God and still occupy a pew? The answer is quite simple. They never read or study their Bible themselves. They allow someone else to read it and tell them what it is saying.

I believe much of the problem lies at the shepherd's feet. So many preachers overlook the need for their people's spiritual growth. The 34th chapter of Ezekiel says God will take the sheep away from the shepherds who do not care for them. *Shepherds BEWARE!* We are not to be as concerned with "our" needs as we are with the needs of "our people."

The last few scriptures above show that this probably speaks of Rome and the Catholic Church, who have brought the compromise. Even more than that, it speaks to individuals in all churches who have compromised themselves.

2 Timothy 3:5. "Having a form of godliness but denying the power thereof: from such turn away."

When a person claims to be a Christian on the outside but who is not on the inside. It's so easy to point to someone else, but in so doing, we should examine ourselves as well. These two verses explain more clearly the entities depicted symbolically as a "woman" and a "beast."

The Beast as an empire goes through four stages, from the viewpoint of the beginning of the Tribulation period."

- It "was"; that is, it existed in the form of the ancient Roman Empire.

- It "is not"; it has not existed as an empire since the fifth century and will not live again until the Antichrist gains worldwide authority during the Tribulation period.

- It "shall ascent out of the bottomless pit," that is, Satan will raise the Antichrist as his false messiah and give him worldwide rule (Revelation 11:7; 13:3-4)

- The Antichrist will be cast into "perdition," the lake of fire (Revelation 19:20). Unbelievers will "wonder" in amazement at this revival of the power and glory of the Roman Empire (Revelation 13:3).

Revelation 17:7: "And the angel said unto me, wherefore did you marvel? I will tell thee the mystery of the woman and the beast that carries her, which hath the seven heads and ten horns."

"Mystery": Not that Babylon is a false system of religion, because that is already known, but that the beast will fully support the harlot and exert vast influence over the whole earth.

The Vision of the Beast

Five details describing the beast are given:

1. Blasphemous names (verse 3).

2. Had seven heads (verse 3).

3. And ten horns (verse 3).

4. The prostitute rides it (verse 7).

5. The beast was and is not and will come out of the bottomless pit (Abyss) and go to his destruction (verse 11).

The careful Bible student will at once recognize this beast even before examining the angel's interpretation. In the first place, it is like the beast (Rev. 13) and doubtless is what all beasts used symbolize: either a king or a kingdom that opposes God's will.

When John sees the great prostitute, he is "greatly astonished?" Some parts of this vision should have been familiar to John, for it is the same beast as that described (chapter 13).

The angel introduces his explanation with the words, "These calls for a mind with wisdom" (verse 9), which shows that only someone with the wisdom of God (found in the Word of God) can understand this vision.

Revelation 17:8: "The beast that thou saw was, and is not; and shall ascend out of the bottomless pit, and go into perdition: and they that dwell on the earth shall wonder, whose names were not written in the book of life from the foundation of the world, when they behold the beast that was and is not, and yet is."

"The beast": Both a king and kingdom are referred to by this term.

"Was and is not; and shall ascend" refers to the Antichrist's false resurrection (13:3-4; 12-14; 13:3).

"Out of the bottomless pit": After his "resurrection," the Antichrist will become owned by a great demon from the abyss (Rev. 13:1, 3).

This mark shows that the power given unto this group comes from the bottomless pit.

Here, it is speaking of the reforming of the old Roman empire. The ten common market nations in Europe reformed the ancient Roman empire. I believe these "ten horns" are the ten common market nations.

The headquarters for these ten nations is in Rome. In 1954, the ten Member States were Belgium, France, Germany, Greece, Italy, Luxembourg, Netherlands, Portugal, Spain, and the United Kingdom.

"Go into perdition": Eternal destruction (Matt. 7:13; John 17:12; Phil. 1:28; 3:19; 2 Thess. 2:3; Heb. 10:39; 2 Peter 2:3; 3:7, 16). It is the lake of fire, the place of Antichrist's destruction (19:20).

"Book of life": The roll of the elect, written in eternity past by God (Revelation 3:5). Only the elect will escape the Antichrist's

deception (Matt. 24:24).

"From the foundation of the world" (Revelation 13:8; 2 Tim. 1:9; Titus 1:2; "long ages ago"). A frequent phrase (Matt. 13:35; 25:34; Luke 11:50; John 17:24; Eph. 1:4; Heb. 4:3; 9:26; 1 Peter 1:20) refers to God's pre-creation plan.

The word *"perdition"* means ruin, loss, or damnable. The Roman Empire was in great power. It fell and then revived again in the ten nations. It is a wonder how Berlin was divided into two parts after World War II. It was done so the line of the old Roman empire would be the same. Of course, the governments of the U.S. and Russia did not know why they did this, but it proved the old territory anyhow.

"The beast that thou saw". Whose names were not written in the Book of life". The false religious system of the end times will be compelling and popular among the unsaved. Still, those who have committed themselves to Christ will understand that anything idolatrous is not of God.

Revelation 17:9: "And here is the mind which hath wisdom. The seven heads are seven mountains, on which the woman sits."

The *"seven heads" of the Beast represent* "seven mountains, on which the woman sits." Rome was known throughout the ancient world as a city built on seven hills or mountains. John notes that the wise "mind" will make the proper identification. The woman is an idolatrous, anti-God civilization centered in Rome but with worldwide influence (verse 15).

The identification of the seven heads as Rome shows that the Beast will also have his significant base of operations at Rome (Dan. 9:26). The "people of the prince that shall come" are the Romans (in A.D. 70).

"Seven mountains": The Greek words often used for hills (Matt. 5:1; 15:29; John 6:15; 8:1). Many commentators interpret this expression to mean Rome, which sits on seven hills. It is true that the final worldwide system of false religion includes, but is not necessarily limited to, Rome. Still, precisely, the seven mountains in

context likely symbolize the seven kingdoms and their kings of verse 10.

We will see in this scripture that the city of Seven Hills is where this evil system has its headquarters. It is a marvel to the world, who are not fully aware of the implications of the Bible. Of course, the bride of Christ, the Christians with their names written in the Lamb's book of life since the world began, are aware of all this and why it happened.

The Antichrist is a copycat. Just as God has a trinity, so does the devil. God's trinity is God the Father, God the Son, and God the Holy Spirit. The Devil's trinity is Antichrist, beast, and false prophet. You see, the false prophet must be involved in leading a church. He will proclaim Jesus on one hand but deny the power on the other.

Interestingly, the Catholic church and the National Council of Churches united in the early 1950s to make the church one physically. God does want us to be one, but not physically.

He wants us to be one in the Spirit. There are people in all churches who will be saved as individuals. We must remove ourselves from the apostate church if possible.

This National Council of churches has come out with a Bible that waters Jesus down to the point that it indicates that Jesus is not God.

It is hazardous. They would have us believe that Jesus was just a man walking down here on earth. My Bible says He was Immanuel, "God with us" (Matthew 1:23).

It says (2 John 1:7), "For many deceivers are entered into the world, who confess not that Jesus Christ is come in the flesh. It is a deceiver and an Antichrist."

In (John 1:14) we read, "And the Word was made flesh, and dwelt among us, (and we beheld his glory, the glory as of the only begotten of the Father,) full of grace and truth."

You see, by all this, that Jesus was, in fact, God the Word, who came and inhabited the body of a man so that it could be possible for

His body to die on the cross for our sins.

Anyone or anything that denies Jesus as God manifests in the flesh is not of God. The sad thing is that most people proclaiming to know Jesus have accepted this new Bible and its teachings.

Whenever you pick up a brochure in Rome, they tell you they are the city of seven hills. The headquarters for the ten common market nations is also here. You see anything that you would like to believe here is in Rome.

The *"wisdom"* of this is that anyone who can read a brochure or hear an advertisement in Rome knows what is spoken of here.

The identification of the seven heads as Rome shows that the Beast will initially have his significant base of operations in Rome.

It is thought by many studying the end times that after the Harlot has been killed, the beast will move his headquarters to the actual city of Babylon during the last three- and one-half years.

Revelation 17:10: "And there are seven kings: five are fallen, and one is, and the other has not yet come; and when he cometh, he must continue a short space."

"Seven kings": Representatives of the seven great world empires (Egypt, Assyria, Babylon, Medo-Persia, Greece, Rome, and that of the Antichrist). Daniel's image in (Dan. 2:37-45).

"Five are fallen, one is, and the other is not yet come.": When John wrote this, the Egyptian, Assyrian, Babylonian, Media-Persian and Greek empires had gone out of existence; Rome still existed, and the Antichrist's empire had not yet come.

When it does, it will be brief (12:12; 13:5), and he will end in perdition (verses 8 & 11).

It could speak of old empires including past kingdoms, such as the Egyptian, Assyrian, Babylonian, Persian, and Greek.

When John wrote this, the Roman government was the power to be, which fell shortly after that and was restored in the ten common market nations banning together, reviving the old Roman empire.

The seven heads of this beast mentioned, according to Tim LaHaye, are kings of the Roman Empire.

The best definition is that there are five kings up to the time of John; the sixth, Domitian, was the Roman king at the time of John, who then skips forward to the end time for the seventh head, which will bring the king of the revived Roman Empire.

The Roman Empire was in great power; it fell and will be revived again.

Then (verse 11) describes the Antichrist, the eighth and final king who will rule the entire world (kingdom).

A rather interesting scripture about the Holy Spirit's description of the beasts that are kingdoms appears in the book of Daniel. When one thinks of world governments, they take on a beautiful shape, as did King Nebuchadnezzar's dream in Daniel.

In his dream, the beast held four different types of metals. Each section of that image represented one of the four coming world kingdoms that were coming at that time (Nebuchadnezzar's Babylon was already there and was the first of the four).

At that time, two governments had already come and gone: Assyria and Egypt.

Those four beasts found (Daniel 2:35) are explained as Daniel interprets Nebuchadnezzar's dream for him. The "four beasts" in his dream is Babylon, represented by the head of gold. The two arms of silver stood for the kingdoms of Media and Persia.

The belly and thighs of brass (or bronze) represented Greece. And the fourth kingdom described the Roman Empire as the legs of iron. When God describes the coming world kingdoms, He uses beasts to symbolize them. Human beings look favorably on government as a great help to them.

In contrast, God looks at the government as a great hindrance to them, as does anyone who has studied history and saw the government's bestial treatment of humanity.

Whether this scripture describes kings or empires doesn't matter; they still mean the same, which makes up the beast described here.

The *seven kingdoms or empires* throughout history that have ruled over Israel and much of the known world are:

(1) Egypt.

(2) Assyria.

(3) Babylon.

(4) Medo-Persia.

(5) Greece.

(6) Rome – The Roman Empire existed at the time of John, which ceased to exist.

(7) And then the seventh, the revived Rome, which had not yet come.

(8) Then the eighth and final will be the Antichrist (verse 8).

It revived Roman Empire is represented in the book of Daniel by the ten toes in the image of (Daniel 2:41-44), and by the ten horns on the fourth beast of Daniel (Dan. 7:7, 20, 24), and in Revelation by the ten horns on the first Beast (13:1; 17:3, 12, 13).

It will only exist as a significant power since it gives authority to the Beast (11-13).

Revelation 17:11: "And the beast that was, and is not, even he is the eighth, and is of the seven, and go into perdition."

"The beast": The final world kingdom ruled by the Antichrist is "the eighth" king or kingdom. He "is of the seven" in that he is the culmination of all the earlier pagan, idolatrous empires. But he will go "into perdition," the lake of fire (verse 8; 19:20).

"Was and is not ... an eighth": The Antichrist's kingdom is said to be both the seventh and eighth kingdoms because of his supposed demise and resurrection. He is the seventh king before and the eighth king after his "resurrection" when he destroys the harlot's religious empire and demands exclusive worship of himself (verse 16).

The beast, the final world kingdom ruled by the Antichrist, is the eighth king or kingdom. He is of the seven in that he is the culmination of all the earlier pagan, idolatrous empires and the reason many think the Antichrist will arise out of the revised Roman Empire. But then he will go into perdition, the lake of fire.

Put another way, the beast that John saw is the Antichrist, the satanic ruler of the last and most powerful empire in human history, who will serve as Satan's instrument to attack Israel, persecute believers, conquer the world for Satan, and oppose Christ.

Scripture portrays him as an intellectual genius (Dan. 7:8), an outstanding orator (Dan. 7:20), a military leader without parallel in human history (Dan. 7:23), a shrewd, calculating, and manipulating politician (Dan 8:25, 11:21), and the ultimate religious charlatan (2 Thess. 2:4). The angel briefly reviews the detailed description of him given (in Rev. 13:1-10).

Verses 12-14: "The ten horns" on the Beast represent "ten kings" of the future revived Roman Empire (Dan. 2:41-44; 7:24). Their worldwide "power" will come in association with the "beast." "One hour" shows a relatively short time (Rev.18:10, 17, 19).

These rulers of a Ten-nation federation will unitedly give their political authority and military power to the beast to conquer the earth and "make war" against Christ (16:14; 19:19).

The purpose of Satan through the Beast and fellow kings is to set up an invincible kingdom that Christ cannot overcome when He returns.

But Christ is "King of" all "kings" and will "overcome" the Beast and his kingdom when He returns (Rev.19:11-21). Those who follow Christ are "called and chosen" by Him and "faithful" to Him (Rev.19:7-8, 14).

Revelation 17:12: "And the ten horns which thou saw are ten kings, which have received no kingdom as yet; but receive power as kings one hour with the beast."

"Ten kings" (Rev.12:3; 13:1; Dan. 2:41-42). These kings were subrulers under the Antichrist, whose empire would be divided into ten administrative districts.

Here, we see that ten separate countries make up this evil group.

Reading (in Daniel 2:45), the ten toes of the fourth beast (Roman Empire) were made of iron and miry clay, creating a brittle substance. It is speaking of the ten kingdoms or kings that will emanate from the Roman Empire and exist at the time of Christ's return. Their worldwide power will come in association with the beast.

It is speaking of the reforming of the old Roman Empire. Ten European common market nations have reformed the ancient Roman Empire.

There are more currently, but only ten will become prominent at the end of time. I believe these "ten horns" are those ten common market nations. The headquarters for these ten nations is in Rome.

These rulers of a ten-nation federation will unite to give the beast their political authority and military power to conquer the earth and make war against Christ (16:14; 19:19).

The purpose of Satan through the Beast and fellow kings is to set up an invincible kingdom that Christ cannot overcome when He returns.

But Christ is King of all kings and will overcome the beast and his kingdom when He returns (19:11-21).

Those who follow Christ are called, chosen, and faithful to Him (19:7-8, 14).

"Which have received no kingdom yet": Thus, the kings cannot be identified with historical figures.

At this point in his career, the Beast will have total control of the world, for he will command ten "kings" who rule the nations of the earth: The ten horns which you saw are ten kings who have received no kingdom as yet, but they receive authority for one hour as kings with the beast.

Revelation 17:13: "These have one mind and shall give their power and strength unto the beast."

These are of one mind "and shall give their power and strength unto the beast." Then, the Beast's kingdom starts to come apart. He hears rumors of insurrection, which fill him "with great fury to destroy and annihilate many," in Daniel's terminology (Dan. 11:44).

It is to fulfill prophecy. Kings and Kingdoms, good and evil, must do indeed what God wants. Sometimes, they are not even aware of why they are doing it. God puts the idea into their head, while all the time, they think it is their clever idea.

He marches to the Valley of Megiddo, where he meets other armies of the world, and there, they do a fantastic thing, as we see in the following scripture.

Revelation 17:14: "These shall make war with the Lamb, and the Lamb shall overcome them: for he is Lord of lords and King of kings: and they that are with him [are] called, and chosen, and faithful."

"Make war": A reference to the battle of Armageddon (16:14-16), where the Lamb will destroy the kings (19:17-21).

Lord of lords, and King of kings": A title for Jesus (19:16; 1 Tim. 6:15; compare Deut. 10:17; Psalm 136:3) that emphasizes His sovereignty over all other rulers to whom He has delegated authority.

"These shall make war with the Lamb." It will occur when these kings kill His faithful followers and come out to fight against Christ in the "Battle of Armageddon." Those who join with Christ to overcome them are called "chosen and faithful," titles used in other Scriptures to describe true believers (1 Pet. 2:9).

You see, as has been said so many times before, we Christians are in a battle. Our leader is the Lamb (Jesus Christ). We are fighting a genuine enemy. The devil and his demons are our enemies.

This war we are in is a war of the spirit. We must come against the devil in hand-to-hand combat every day. Our weapon is the two-edged sword (Bible).

This war is fought by an army of believers who always have their weapons (Bible) at their side. Besides having it at their side, they have its contents inside them (their food is the Word of God). When they are in hot combat, the sword comes from their mouth. They are willing to lay down their lives for the cause of Jesus.

The flag we Christian's fly is the banner of righteousness. It is red because of our leader's blood, white because of the righteousness of believers, and blue for our heavenly calling. It is a voluntary army. This battle is in the final hours before the return of the Lord. This army will include boys, girls, men, and women. God has called a vast army, as He did in Gideon's day.

This group will be sold out completely to God. They will be willing to give up homes, family, friends, wealth, and position in their community to work for God. They will be loyal to Jesus even to the death. They will have a peculiar uniform described (in Ephesians chapter 6, this is the Christian's armor).

This uniform will be provided to us by our Lord (Jesus). Loins girded about with truth, the breastplate of righteousness, feet shod with the preparation of the gospel, the shield of faith, the helmet of salvation, and the sword of the Spirit, the Word of God.

The big difference is that this army will have patches on their knees. This battle will be fought with much prayer (on our knees). You see, this victory is the Lord's. We must fight the good fight. Give it everything you have. The war is peaking now. God needs good Christians who will not compromise for any reason. The battle is hard, but the rewards are beyond comprehension: a home in heaven forever with Jesus and the opportunity to hear Him say, "Well done, thy good and faithful servant."

We soldiers shall be kings and priests (Rev. 1:6; Rev 5:10), but He will be Lord and King overall. We are called, chosen, and faithful. Hallelujah! Verses 15-18: "The whore" has been described as sitting.

(1) On many "waters" (verse 1);

(2) On the Beast (verse 3); and

(3) On seven mountains (verse 9).

Revelation 17:15 "And he saith unto me, the waters which thou saw, where the whore sit, are peoples, and multitudes, and nations, and tongues."

Here, the waters are identified as "peoples, and multitudes, and nations, and tongues," showing the worldwide influence and authority of the harlot. (In verse 18), she is identified as "that great city, which reigned over the kings of the earth," referring probably to a worldwide, idolatrous pagan system centered in Rome

The Prostitute Explained. Then the angel explains to John the meaning of the water on which the woman is sitting: It is the people of the earth. In Revelation, people, multitudes, nations, and languages constitute all humanity. As in the saying, *"sea of humanity".*

Those who are followers of the evil system will be from all nations. There will be hundreds of millions lost.

Revelation 17:16 "And the ten horns which thou saw upon the beast, these shall hate the whore, and shall make her desolate and naked, and shall eat her flesh, and burn her with fire."

"These shall hate the whore": After using the false religious system to unify the world kingdoms and gain control of all, the Antichrist, with the help of his ten sub-rulers, will turn against the system, take and destroy it, and seize all power and worship for himself. They will fulfill God's will (verse 17; Gen. 50:20).

The Coming Destruction of the Babylonian Prostitute ("Babylon the Harlot"). The Antichrist will allow the one world (apostate) church to govern his actions during the first three- and one-half years of the Tribulation while he is gathering more and more power (see article "One World Religion").

But in the middle of the Tribulation, when he feels he can become an autocratic ruler, he and the ten kings throw off the prostitute because while being dominated by her, they "hate the prostitute."

None of the world's political leaders have enjoyed subjugation to religious leaders but have continued in a servile role only for expediency.

When it is no longer necessary, the ten kings will "bring her to ruin and leave her naked," meaning they will confiscate her temples, her gold, and her costly apparel. In so doing, they will unwittingly be the instruments of God in destroying this awful Babylonian system once and for all: "For God has put it into their hearts to accomplish his purpose."

Here, we see these evil ten nations turning against the world and the world church. This power, these wicked nations, have been and are being used to rule the little people. This fire speaks of war. These ten nations will do away with this church, even though it is the apostate church.

When Will the Prostitute Religion Be Destroyed? The religious Babylon (Rev. 17), which is destroyed, comes in two parts. One occurs during the first part of the Tribulation when the governmental system of Babylon (pictured as this ugly "beast") is gaining world control but must allow the *"prostitute" to sit on and ride the beast.*

We see this as meaning she exercises a degree of control over the Babylonian system by bringing the world's nations under her idolatrous religious power.

During the first half of the Tribulation, she incurs the wrath of the ten kings who see her use the authority of the Antichrist to advance her religious causes. So, they plot to kill her. The reason we know this killing of the prostitute of "mystery Babylon" is done in the middle of the Tribulation is twofold:

(1) "The deadly wound" of the Antichrist is healed by the indwelling of Satan himself, simulating the resurrection of Christ in the middle of the Tribulation.

(2) From then on, the world did not worship Babylon's mystery but the beast's image. The False Prophet will do away with all religion except the worship of Antichrist Satan, which he will enforce. That begins at the beginning of the Great Tribulation, which is described (Rev.13).

It is when people will have to take the mark of the beast and swear their loyalty to it or face death. There is no middle ground; either accept Jesus or accept the beast.

Since the woman who rides the beast gets her authority from the beast, the Holy Spirit uses this description to show how religious Babylon and governmental Babylon are so intertwined they are presented together. However, they are destroyed at different times.

The prostitute (spiritual Babylon) is destroyed by the "beast and the kings of the earth," who "hate the prostitute" and kill her.

It clears the way for the Antichrist to fulfill the lifetime dream of Satan to get people to worship him. She is destroyed in the middle of the Tribulation. Then, the governmental system will be destroyed at the end of the Great Tribulation when commercial Babylon is destroyed (Rev. 18).

With _"Mystery Babylon the mother of Prostitutes" out of the way,_ "all inhabitants of the earth will worship the beast, all whose names have not been written in the book of life belonging to the Lamb that was slain from the creation of the world" (Rev. 13:8).

Religious Babylon Destroyed. Archaeologists tell us that Babylon is the cradle of civilization. Located on the Euphrates River's shores, this city's ruins have revealed some of the most ancient documents of past generations. This city, begun by Nimrod, who was a rebel before the Lord, authored some of the greatest evils ever to fall on humankind.

Two of these evils will be destroyed during the Tribulation period, according to (Rev. 17;18).

In ancient days, Satan seemed to make Babylon the capital of this evil operation. From this headquarters was started false religion, humanity's attempt for self-government in defiance of God's will and city dwellings for commercial and social purposes contrary to God's command to "be fruitful and increase in number and fill the earth." (Gen. 1:28). These great evils, which have damned the souls of millions by substituting counterfeit solutions to natural human problems that would ordinarily lead a person to God, will all be destroyed at the end of the Tribulation period.

Chapter 17 describes the judgment of God on the religious system that has enslaved humanity in superstitious darkness for centuries.

Revelation 17:17: "For God hath put in their hearts to fulfill his will, and to agree, and give their kingdom unto the beast until the words of God shall be fulfilled."

Toward the end of the Tribulation period, however, the ten kings (verse 12) will destroy the harlot system (Rev. 18:6-24). They will do this as God's "will" and will turn their total devotion and worship to the "beast" himself (Rev.13:12; 17:13; Dan. 11:36-39). The ten kings will be God's instrument to destroy the harlot Babylon (Rev.16:19; 18:5-6; 19:2). The destruction of the "woman" or harlot is pictured as the destruction of a "great city" (Rev. 18).

You see, all are subject to God, whether following the beast or God. Even the devil must do exactly what God tells him to do. Some of this has happened to fulfill God's word. The devil is not only subject to God, but he is subject to us, as well, through the mighty name of Jesus.

We may dismiss the devil, just as Jesus did. The only difference was that Jesus used His power, and we have no authority. We do it in the name of Jesus. It is Jesus' power.

Revelation 17:18: "And the woman which thou saw is that great city, which reigned over the kings of the earth."

"Great city": Here is another identification of the capital city of Babylon, the centerpiece of Antichrist's empire (Rev. 18:10, 18, 21).

Many have taken this to mean that the woman stands for the capital city of Antichrist's kingdom, but this cannot be, for Antichrist rules over the earth's kings.

If the woman is not the Antichrist, what other possible explanation can we have for such unanimous world dominance? The only answer is the one system before which all kings, dictators, and nations have been forced to bow down throughout history, that is, the Babylonian religion of idolatry. One cannot go anywhere without being confronted with some semblance of idolatry.

No system in the world's history has enslaved more people than this awful religion. It should not take us by surprise that this prostitute woman, the religious system, is referred to as a city.

When used symbolically, a woman is always intended to signify a spiritual or religious movement throughout the Scripture. If a good woman, it is "Jehovah's wife" or "the bride of Christ."

If an evil woman, such as "a prostitute," it stands for the corrupt religious system of idolatry. Here, we see Rome again. In its heyday, Rome was considered the world's capital. They, indeed, did reign over all of Europe.

We conclude then that Revelation 17 describes the destruction of the religious system. In contrast, Revelation 18 denotes the destruction of "Satan's seat," the commercial and governmental city of Babylon, marking the prelude to the consummation of the Tribulation.

No longer does the seer John has the ecclesiastical religious system in view but now turns the spotlight of God's judgment on the commercial and governmental systems that originated there. Babylon has had the most harmful effect on humanity of all the world's cities.

For all idolatrous religion, greed-based commerce, and secular government were begun there. At the end of the Tribulation, God will destroy them all in the seventh or last vial judgment to fulfill the prophecy (Isaiah 47:1-9; 21:9).

CHAPTER 14
REVELATION 18

Commercial and Political Babylon is now in view. The destruction of religious Babylon described (in Rev. 17), and commercial Babylon here (in chapter 18) will decisively rid the world of the principal evils that have plagued humanity for about 5000 years. We have already seen the destruction to be unleashed on ecclesiastical or religious Babylon at the beginning of the Great Tribulation period.

However, the destruction of the commercial and governmental systems will not occur until the end of the Great Tribulation. Some Bible scholars do not distinguish between the collapse of Chapter seventeen and Chapter eighteen but mold them all together. The following six reasons establish that they are not the same.

"After these things" (Rev 18:1), this expression shows that the events described (chapter 18) will not take place until after the events of chapter 17 have been fulfilled.

"I saw another angel coming down from heaven." Events of chapter 17 were introduced by "one of the seven angels who had the seven bowls" (Rev 17:1). The angel referred to (chapter 18) is not the same as the one who introduced the events of chapter seventeen.

Therefore, we can expect the same events throughout Revelation: When an angel fulfills his responsibility, another distinct judgment occurs on earth.

The names in the two chapters are different. The title in chapter 18 is "Babylon the Great" (Rev. 18:2). True, Babylon destroyed in chapter 17 has the name, "Mystery, Babylon the Great, the mother of Prostitutes and the Abominations of the whole Earth" (Rev. 17:5).

But the only similarity is the location, Babylon. When both titles are used fully, the contrast between these two Babylon's is seen.

Babylon, the prostitute of chapter seventeen, will be destroyed by the kings of the earth (Rev. 17:16). The cataclysmic judgments of God will destroy the Babylon of chapter 18.

The kings who destroy the Babylon of chapter seventeen rejoice. In the Babylon of chapter 18, the kings and merchants lament and weep for her (Rev. 18:9-15).

Suppose chapters seventeen and eighteen occur during the last days of the Great Tribulation. In that case, there will be no place for the Antichrist and the False Prophet to do away with all religions and substitute the worship of the Antichrist's image as described (Rev.13).

Verses 1-3: That the city "Babylon" in chapter 18 is the same as the whore or harlot in chapter 17 is shown by:

(1) The parallels between the two (17:1-6, 15-18 with 18:2-3, 6-8, 12, 18-24).

(2) The identification of the harlot as the "great city" in 17:18.

(3) The summary of Babylon's judgment in 19:2-3; and

(4) The fact that the imagery in both chapters comes from Old Testament references to Tyre, Nineveh, and Babylon (compare Isa. Chapters 13, 14, and 23: Ezek. chapters 26-28; Jer. chapters 50-51).

The language of chapter 18 is highly figurative. The phrase "after these things" shows that chapter 18 is a further revelation concerning Babylon: the results of her destruction. (verse 2), her doom is announced: "Babylon the great is fallen" (Isa. 21:9).

The reference to "devils" (demons) and "every foul spirit" shows the destruction and utter desolation of the harlot system. "All nations": The "merchants of the earth" have become wealthy through the apostate, idolatrous system centered in Rome.

Revelation 18:1: "And after these things I saw another angel come down from heaven, having great power; and the earth was lightened with his glory."

Then John saw another angel coming down from heaven. We are not told whether "another angel" is one of the seven angels with the seven vials. But it seems doubtful, for this angel is distinctive, with such "great authority" that he lights the earth with his glory.

"Earth was lightened with his glory": The fifth vial (16:10) will have plunged the world into darkness. Against that backdrop, another angel's sudden, blazing appearance (17:1, 7, 15) will undoubtedly rivet the world's attention on him and his message of judgment on Babylon (14:8).

In the last lesson, we saw that the beast, his system, and the great whore were revealed. Here, in chapter 18, we will see the judgment that comes from God poured out on them. This "angel" (in verse 1) was sent from heaven. This "power" spoken of here is the power God endowed on this angel to execute this punishment. This "angel" has been in close association with the Light. We see here that this potent Light of Jesus, even though second-hand through the angel, still lightens the earth.

Revelation 18:2: "And he cried mightily with a strong voice, saying, Babylon the great is fallen, is fallen, and is become the habitation of devils, and the hold of every foul spirit, and a cage of every unclean and hateful bird."

"Babylon the great is fallen" (14:8; Isa. 21:9), the verse from which these words come. The Greek text views these results as if they had already taken place (14:8). But the seventh vial is being referred to here and is yet to come (16:17-21). When it comes, devastation and destruction will occur, leaving the place to demons.

The message of this angel who cries with a "mighty voice" is this: "Fallen! Fallen is Babylon the Great!" Since chapter eighteen seems to describe the destruction of a literal commercial city, the governmental capital of the world, during the Tribulation, we naturally ask ourselves, "Where is that city?" Again, Bible prophecy students are not in agreement. Some suggested the city of Rome, and some years ago, he told New York City because he felt it was the world's commercial center.

Some who believe we should take the Scriptures literally whenever possible are inclined to think that the city of Babylon will be rebuilt.

There is a similar description of this very same thing in Isaiah:

Isaiah 21:9: "And, behold, here cometh a chariot of men, with a couple of horsemen. And he answered and said, Babylon is fallen, is fallen; and all the graven images of her gods he hath broken unto the ground."

Here, we see the fall of the great apostate church. We also know the fall of these ten evil nations. God is not mocked. God wins the war. God has given up on them completely. Now judgment comes. Babylon is a hostile group, but they are not the world.

They are the church gone bad. For a while, the world and the apostate church walked together. The evil ten nations, at last, have turned against this apostate church, both Catholic and Protestant. It is the church that has committed spiritual adultery. Iraq is physical Babylon.

This _"...strong voice... came from God._ In this apostate church, God doesn't even claim anymore. The real Christians are already in heaven. Now we see even this watered-down church fall, which leaves the way open for every unclean spirit. Demons control.

In (Rev. 18:10, 16, 18, 19, and 21), you find a reference to this Babylon being a city. (In verse 2), the angel cried mightily and said, "Babylon the Great **is fallen, is fallen** "A literal" interpretation would dictate that this Babylon is a city. But I do not believe this is so! If you read (Rev. 17:18), you see: "And the woman which thou saw is that great city, which reigns over the Kings of the earth."

The "woman" was the corrupt religious system and not a city. The same applies here. Commercial Babylon is a corrupt commercial, social, and political system that will be destroyed at the end of the Tribulation. Read the six reasons given before verse one of this chapter again.

Revelation 18:3: "For all nations have drunk of the wine of the wrath of her fornication, and the kings of the earth have committed fornication with her, and the merchants of the earth are waxed rich through the abundance of her delicacies."

"Wine of the wrath of her fornication": Religious Babylon (chapter 17) lures the nations into spiritual drunkenness and fornication with false gods (17:2, 4); commercial Babylon (chapter 18) seduces the unbelieving world into a materialistic stupor so that the people of the world will become drunk with passion because of their relationship with Babylon.

"Kings ... merchants": Political rulers and corporate leaders alike are swept up in this worldwide system of commerce (14:8; 17:2).

Remember, in chapter 16, we saw the actual destruction of commercial Babylon. At the end of this chapter, I will show it again so you can understand what is happening.

The corruption may have begun in Babylon, but it has spread to every corner of the earth. It will not be until the world is destroyed that this evil will be no more. Those who mourn are losing their ability to deceive the nations any longer.

Looking ahead at what it says in:

Rev. 18:23: "For thy merchants were the great men of the earth; for by thy sorceries were all nations deceived."

So, you see, this is not a city but a very corrupt system that is being destroyed by God by his Judgment to prepare for the coming

Kingdom of our Lord Jesus Christ.

Verses 4-8: Believers must be separate from the harlot system, or they may be found to share in "her sins" and thereby "receive" part of her judgment. "God hath remembered her iniquities":

The day of judgment for sin has arrived. The "double" judgment emphasizes full punishment for her sins (Jer. 16:18; 17:18; 50:29). That she calls herself a "queen" and "no widow" shows her arrogant selfconfidence (Isa. 47:7-8).

She sees herself as beyond any possibility of personal "sorrow." But the humbling of the harlot (Luke 14:11) will involve "torment" and "sorrow."

"One day" may be a literal day or a symbol of sudden destruction. The "fire" may also be either literal fire or a sign of the judgment of God (Jer. 51:25-58). It is reminiscent of the burning of Rome in A.D. 64 by Nero.

Revelation 18:4: "And I heard another voice from heaven, saying, come out of her, my people, that ye be not partakers of her sins, and that ye receive not of her plagues."

"Come out of here, my people": God will call His own to disentangle themselves from this evil system. It may also be God's calling for the elect to abandon the world system and believe in the Savior. In either case, the message is to leave the system before it is destroyed (2 Cor. 6:17; 1 John 2:15). The judgment of God on that society living in sinful, arrogant selfindulgence can be avoided. Isaiah's and Jeremiah's gave a message to their people to leave Babylon (Isa. 48:20; Jer. 50:8; 51:6-9, 45). In both cases, the message is to abandon the system.

Read (2 Cor. 6:14-17) below for an excellent example of this:

(14) Be ye not unequally yoked with unbelievers: for what fellowship hath righteousness with unrighteousness? and what communion hath light with darkness?

(15) And what concord had Christ with Belial? or what part hath he that believeth with an infidel?

(16) And what agreement hath the temple of God with idols? For ye are the temple of the living God; as God said, I will dwell in them, and walk in them; I will be their God, and they shall be my people.

(17) Wherefore come out from among them, and be ye separate, saith the Lord, and touch not the unclean thing; and I will receive you,

True believers, who are still in this type of church, are very foolish. Through this "voice from heaven," God says, "Come out of here, my people." It is not speaking of Rome but the apostate church. His people are the church. He leaves no doubt what a person should do if caught in these apostate churches.

You see, even though you are not sinning, as such. You are sinning by association. The Bible repeatedly tells us not to be unequally yoked with those of unbelief. If you do not remove yourself, you are guilty of her sin. In (verse 4), we read that her plagues will also come to you.

If your church preaches that Jesus was not born of a virgin, or the Red Sea did not part, that a whale did not swallow Jonah, or if your church recognizes homosexuals and lesbians as equals and does not condemn it as sin, you had better get out. No one or nothing should be put ahead of God. There is no mediator between man and almighty god except Jesus.

1 Timothy 2:5: "For there is one God, and one mediator between God and men, the man Christ Jesus;"

We should not bow down to graven images of anyone or anything. We read in Exodus 20:4 one of the Commandments of God.

Exodus 20:4: "Thou shalt not make unto thee any graven image or any likeness of anything that is in heaven above, or that is in the earth beneath, or that is in the water under the earth:"

Be careful how you worship. Be cautious about the things of God. Know who Jesus is and why you worship Him. Be thoroughly convinced in your heart. Do not listen to someone telling you what the Bible says. Read and study it for yourself. If you try to learn, God will reveal what it says. Even check out what I am saying. Do not be easily swayed by anyone. Be wise as a serpent and harmless as a dove.

The righteous God of the universe has not overlooked the sins of the elite power brokers who have used commerce and government for centuries to live luxuriously at the expense of others. The Antichrist's commercial, social, and political systems will receive double judgment for their sins.

Revelation 18:5: "For her sins have reached unto heaven, and God hath remembered her iniquities."

"Remembered": (16:19). God does not remember the iniquities of His people (Jer. 31:34) but does remember to protect them (Mal. 3:16 – 4:2). For unrepentant Babylon, there will be no such forgiveness, only judgment.

Babylon's sins will pile up like a new Tower of Babel, but unlike the ancient tower, her sins will reach as high as heaven.

Then, an angel states that God has remembered her sins. He will take note of them as He did that earlier monument to man's sinful, arrogant, prideful rebellion at Babel.

It is always good to remember that Revelation was addressed to the church. God gives us warnings and gives us time to repent. Even now, when He has already passed judgment on this apostate church, He is crying out for individuals to come out of this apostate church. Jesus calls us all to righteousness and holiness in Him. It is up to us to answer that call.

Verses 6-7: "Reward her": The angel calls for God to recompense wrath to Babylon in her cup to repay her according to her deeds (see note on 17:4). This is an echo of the Old Testament law of retaliation (Exodus 21:24), which will be implemented by God (Rom. 12:17-

21).

Revelation 18:6: "Reward her even as she rewarded you, and double unto her double according to her works: in the cup which she hath *filled fill to her double.*"

"Double": Has the sense of "full" or "overflowing." The punishment will fit the crime (Jer. 16:18).

"Cup": The cup of wickedness from which so many have drunk (14:8; 17:2, 4, 6) will call for the cup of wrath (14:10; 16:19).

They reward her" simply means will recompense or repay commercial Babylon according to her works. All of those who are involved and are guilty will suffer double judgment as the cup is filled twice for her for what she has done to the Saints ("Babylon the City").

She will reap what she sowed.

Revelation 18:7: "How much she hath glorified herself, and lived deliciously, so much torment and sorrow give her: for she saith in her heart, I sit a queen, and am no widow, and shall see no sorrow."

"And am no widow": A proud but empty boast of self-sufficiency made by historical Babylon (Isa. 47:8; 1 Cor. 10:12).

It describes three sins she is guilty of.

(1) "She has glorified herself," meaning she is proud.

(2) "She lived Deliciously," meaning she pursued self-gratification.

(3) "I sit a queen, and am no widow, and shall see no sorrow," meaning she was proud and boastful.

That proud boast echoes that of ancient Babylon, who said, "I will be a queen forever," I will not sit as a widow nor know the loss of children. Now read that boast (Isaiah 47):

Isaiah 47:7-8 "And thou said I shall be a lady forever: so that thou didst not lay these things to thy heart, neither didst remember the latter end of it." "Therefore, hear now this, [thou that art] given to pleasures, that dwellest carelessly, that sayest in thine heart, I am, and no one else besides me; I shall not sit as a widow, neither shall I know the loss of children."

Revelation 18:8: "Therefore shall her plagues come in one day, death, and mourning, and famine; and she shall be utterly burned with fire: for strong is the Lord God who judges her."

"Her plagues": These could include those (16:1) but must be the extraordinary destruction of the city as well, described as "plagues and mourning and famine."

"In one day" (verses 10, 17, 19). The particular judgments on Babylon take place in a brief period. (Daniel 5:30), records that Babylon of old fell in one day.

Isaiah 47:9: "But these two things shall come to thee in a moment in one day, the loss of children, and widowhood: they shall come upon thee in their perfection for the multitude of thy sorceries and the great abundance of thine enchantments."

It is said that Babylon's destruction will not be progressive. The wicked city system will be instantly destroyed. (Dan 5:25-28, 30), records a similar fate that befell ancient Babylon; the city fell the very night God wrote its doom on the wall of the king's palace.

Babylon's doom is unavoidable and cannot be avoided. As Nebuchadnezzar discovered in Daniel, no one can change God's plans or keep Him from carrying out what He intended. Or, in this case, his grandson Belshazzar (Dan. 5:13-30).

Verses 9-20: This section records the lament over Babylon's destruction, not her sin, by those who were part of her system.

These verses consist of three laments over the fallen city of Babylon, from the perspective of kings (verses 9-10), merchants (verses 11-16), and seamen (verses 17-19; Ezek. chapter 27), followed by a call for rejoicing on the part of God's people and His angels (verse 20).

The "kings" (of verse 9) are not the kings (represented by horns of 17:16) but somewhat various earthly kings who have taken part in the Babylonian system. The laments picture utter chaos on the earth at the end of the Tribulation period.

The "merchants" will find nothing to buy or sell. "In one hour": The destruction will come suddenly and quickly (verse 17). The world's pagan economic system will collapse. "

They cast dust on their heads" as a sign of mourning and sorrow (verse 19; Job 2:12; Lam. 2:10; Ezek. 27:30). "God hath avenged you on her":

God, at last, judges the Babylonian system for its treatment of God's people, particularly those who are martyred during the Tribulation (6:9- 11). Verse 20 shows heaven's perspective on the judgment.

Revelation 18:9: "And the kings of the earth, who have committed fornication and lived deliciously with her, shall bewail her, and lament for her when they shall see the smoke of her burning."

"Kings": The world's political leaders will weep because the loss of their capital city will signal the doom of the Antichrist's empire and the source of their power (verse 3; 17:2).

"Bewail her, and lament for her": Bewail means to weep, and "Weep" means "to sob openly." "Lament" translates the same Greek word used to express the despair of the unbelieving world at the return of Christ (1:7).

It will undoubtedly include the 10 kings of the earth who rule Antichrist's kingdom under his authority and the rest of the world's leaders.

The destruction of the Antichrist's political and economic power will strike a fatal blow to his empire. The fall of Babylon will symbolize the fall of the entire evil world system.

And again, Babylon is pictured as a harlot whose death causes her lovers to weep and lament over her.

Revelation 18:10: "Standing afar off for fear of her torment, saying, Alas, alas, that great city Babylon, that mighty city! for in one hour is thy judgment come."

The "standing afar off" could mean those who heeded and came out of her. It doesn't matter were. It may be all these cities and many more, or it might not be a literal city. I believe this is both an evil system and many evil towns are also being destroyed.

The one hour means the judgment will happen rapidly, just as verse 8 predicted (verses 8, 17, 19).

Revelation 18:11: "And the merchants of the earth shall weep and mourn over her; for no man buy their merchandise anymore."

These mourners are the merchants of the earth who will weep and mourn over Babylon because no one can buy their goods anymore.

Whatever economy there had been would end, and so would any semblance of normalcy on this devastated planet that was already in serious trouble brought on by the divine judgments of God.

Verses 12-13: Over half of their commodities appear in the list (Ezek. 27:12-22).

Revelation 18:12: "The merchandise of gold, and silver, and precious stones, and pearls, and fine linen, and purple, and silk, and scarlet, and all thyine wood, and all manner vessels of ivory, and all manner vessels of most precious wood, and brass, and iron, and marble,"

"Purple" refers to garments laboriously dyed with purple dye extracted from shellfish. Lydia (Acts 16:14) was a seller of such expensive clothes. A distinctive mark of Caesars was their purple robes.

"Thyine wood": Wood from North African citrus trees, highly valued because of its color, which was used to make costly pieces of furniture.

"Marble": Marble, imported from Africa, Egypt, and Greece, was widely used in Roman buildings.

It appears that these are classed into several types:

(1) Personal items of jewelry.

(2) Articles used for furniture.

(3) Nice smelling and tasting things.

(4) Food.

(5) Animals.

(6) Souls of men.

I do not know what significance this has unless it means worldly things. Most of these are things a person could do without if hard times came and you had to, even maybe the food for a while.

The souls of men" is one of the more interesting. In the old Roman Empire days, they sold people as you would animals. Perhaps that is what is meant there. They thought no more about selling a person than they did a pair of shoes.

In all of this, it appears that trade has just about ceased. Probably, all the plagues and wars have just about stopped everything.

Revelation 18:13: "And cinnamon, and odors, and ointments, and frankincense, and wine, and oil, and fine flour, and wheat, and beasts, and sheep, and horses, and chariots, and slaves, and souls of men."

"Ointments" (Matt. 26:7, 12; John 12:3).

"Frankincense": A fragrant gum or resin imported from Arabia

and used in incense and perfume (SOS 3:6; Matt. 2:11).

Enslaved people, and souls of men": The slave trade, long banned by the civilized nations of the world, will reappear in Antichrist's debauched commercial system.

Revelation 18:14: "And the fruits that thy soul lusted after are departed from thee, and all things which were dainty and goodly are departed from thee, and thou shalt find them no more at all."

And the merchandise that was available before is now gone and will never be available again. The commercial system is completely shut down, and that reality is about to be made manifest.

It will probably be a time when it will be next to impossible even to find enough to feed your family. Even if you did find enough for them to eat, it would probably take all you could make to have bread for your family.

It is probably when a loaf of bread would cost a whole day's wages. There will be no money at all left for niceties. Even if you have a tremendous amount of money, there will be significant shortages of exact items necessary to live, and the things the rich consume will be entirely unavailable.

Revelation 18:15: "The merchants of these things, which were made rich by her, shall stand afar off for fear of her torment, weeping and wailing,"

Here, we see great fear from these merchants who used to sell their merchandise at tremendous, outrageous profits. Like today, many get rich from oil by exploiting those who can't afford the inflated prices. And that includes the government, which adds very high taxes to every gallon of gas. When this horrible punishment comes, it will put the fear of God on those looking on. It is about time that someone begins to fear.

These merchants weep because their materialistic passions can no longer be fulfilled. The weeping that begins then will last for eternity in hell. These greedy merchants are a classic illustration of those of all times who gain the whole world only to end up giving up their souls.

Revelation 18:16: "And saying, Alas, alas, that great city, that was clothed in fine linen, and purple, and scarlet, and decked with gold, precious stones, and pearls!"

Any city we would come up with would be pure speculation. As in the earlier lesson, we must realize that "Babylon" is a city and the apostate church. These plagues jump back and forth from the town to the church ("Babylon the City").

The fine linen" has to do with the church world. All of this describes the finery in these big churches. "Purple and scarlet" are Godly colors.

These commodities were common commodities in the ancient world and were the source of immense financial gain. Those materialistic, unrepentant people mourn as God brings His judgment against Babylon, knowing these items will never be found again.

Revelation 18:17: "For in one hour so great riches come to naught. And every shipmaster, and all the company in ships, and sailors, and as many as trade by sea, stood afar off,"

In one Hour, the destruction will come suddenly and quickly. The world's pagan economic system will collapse. They cast dust on their heads as a sign of mourning and sorrow (verse 19, Job. 2:12; Lam. 2:10; Ezek. 27:30). God hath avenged you on her: God at last judges the Babylonian system for its treatment of God's people, particularly those who are martyred during the Tribulation (Rev. 6:9-11).

"Shipmaster": Ship captains will mourn the loss of Babylon and the lucrative transport business that went with it.

Revelation 18:18: "And cried when they saw the smoke of her burning, saying, what city is like unto this great city!"

The people cry and are amazed as they see this destruction before their eyes.

Revelation 18:19: "And they cast dust on their heads, and cried, weeping and wailing, saying, Alas, alas, that great city, wherein were made rich all that had ships in the sea because of her costliness! for in one hour is she made desolate."

Casting dust on their heads is a typical ancient expression of grief. These last few scriptures state sailors but could mean any transportation and delivery systems today, such as planes, trains, trucks, etc. All these services would be shut down at once if the commercial system, including banking and computers, were destroyed.

Even a lukewarm church would undoubtedly be aware of what other believers thought the Bible teaches about the wrath of God. When they realize they have missed the rapture of the Church, there would be grief beyond comprehension. It was a sudden destruction that no one could deny was a punishment from God.

"In one hour": Not just 60 minutes, but one brief period of swift judgment. Consider what would happen if there was no more electrical system available.

Revelation 18:20: "Rejoice over her, thou heaven, and ye holy apostles and prophets; for God hath avenged you on her."

"God hath avenged you on her": The angel will preach the tribulation martyrs (6:9-11) to rejoice, not over the deaths of those doomed to eternal hell, but because God's righteousness and justice will have prevailed.

God has taken vengeance on the ones who killed his prophets and apostles and even his blessed Son. Finally, all of those martyred by these have been avenged.

The long-awaited moment of vindication, retribution, and vengeance for which the martyred tribulation believers had prayed (Rev. 6:9-10), and for which all the redeemed have hoped, that time has arrived.

Verses 21-24: These verses picture the results of the collapse of the Babylonian system from within. The finality of its destruction is shown by the sixfold repetition of the phrase "no more at all." The "stone" cast "into the sea' depicts the "violence" and permanence of the destruction.

The Babylonian system began (in Genesis 10) and has continued uninterrupted in one form or another to the present day. But one day, it will suddenly "sink," never to return.

Revelation 18:21: "And a mighty angel took up a stone like a great millstone, and cast it into the sea, saying, thus with violence shall that great city Babylon be thrown down, and shall be found no more at all."

"Great millstone": Millstones were large, heavy stones used to grind grain. This metaphor portrays the violence of Babylon's overthrow (Jer. 51:61-64; Matt. 18:6).

"Sea" sometimes means masses of people, but I do not believe that is the meaning here. Whether this is only an actual city (rebuilt Babylon) or a sinful commercial, social, and political system that corrupts the entire world, which is being destroyed here, this is speaking of destruction.

More than likely, this is speaking of both, as the two can be easily associated. This millstone is like the one spoken of as being around a neck and thrown into the sea. (Luke 17:1-2).

In the light of this Scripture, this is a dire punishment. I believe this illustration shows the finality of God's judgment. We must remember that God, not the devil, destroys Babylon.

Verses 22-23: The fall of Babylon ends whatever semblance of normalcy will still exist in the world after all the seals, trumpets, and vials. Life will be disrupted, and the end near. However, there is no more music, no industry, no preparing of food ("millstone"), no more power for light, and no more weddings because God will destroy the deceivers and deceived.

Revelation 18:22: "And the voice of harpers, and musicians, and of pipers, and trumpeters, shall be heard no more at all in thee; and no craftsman shall be found any more in thee, and the sound of a millstone shall be heard no more at all in thee;"

Everything grinds to a halt everywhere. As the Old Testament prophets predicted, Babylon will be destroyed so thoroughly that it will never rise again.

Isaiah 13:19-21 "And Babylon, the glory of kingdoms, the beauty of the Chaldees' excellency, shall be as when God overthrew Sodom and Gomorrah." "It shall never be inhabited, neither shall it be dwelt in from generation to generation: neither shall the Arabian pitch tent there; neither shall the shepherds make their fold there." "But wild beasts of the desert shall lie there, and their houses shall be full of doleful creatures, and owls shall dwell there, and satyrs shall dance there."

In (verses 23-24), three reasons are given for the destruction of Babylon:

(1) It's arrogance.

(2) Its deception of the nations; and

(3) Its persecution and martyrdom of God's people.

Revelation 18:23: "And the light of a candle shall shine no more at all in thee; and the voice of the bridegroom and the bride shall be heard no more at all in thee: for thy merchants were the great men of the earth; for by thy sorceries were all nations deceived."

Three final reasons are given for Babylon's judgment. Notice that the merchants are mentioned as the great men of the earth.

1. That's why this is talking of a commercial system as well as a political system. They are not from the city of Babylon but from all parts of the earth.

2. They use their wealth to ascend to positions of power, prominence, and influence. The abuses of the proud, arrogant rich are well documented in scripture. James, Isaiah, and Amos condemned the rich for their self-aggrandizement and maltreatment of the poor.

3. *All the nations were deceived by her sorcery. Sorcery is* from pharmacies, the root word of the English words "pharmacy" and "pharmaceuticals." The phrase is used in the New Testament to refer to magic and occult practices (Gal. 5:20).

We know that "sorceries" have to do with drugs. It seems this city was dealing in drugs. Of course, nearly every major city in the world is also. It is no help in deciding which city. It just helps us prove the extent of the evil. I still believe this city has worldwide connections to a church branch. I genuinely think the deception they brought to the world was spiritual. Here again, the things mentioned that have stopped are every day in all large cities. Babylon's hold on the world will not be entirely due to her military and economic power but also to her occult influence.

Revelation 18:24: "And in her was found the blood of prophets, and of saints, and of all that were slain upon the earth."

A final reason given for Babylon's judgment is her murderous slaughter of God's people.

"Blood of prophets and saints": The religious and commercial/political systems embodied in Babylon will commit unspeakable atrocities against God's people (6:10; 11:7; 13:7, 15; 17:6; 19:2). God will avenge that slaughter of His people (19:2).

It is the city of Babylon and the faithless church as well. True, faithful Christians are often neglected and even oppressed by the church. We see youth lost because of the shallow teachings of this apostate church.

Every time I see strong Christians ridiculed by lukewarm Christians; I am more convinced that more people are lost going to a watered-down church than by not going to church at all. At least those who do not go are not fooled into a false sense of security. They know they are lost.

Reaching someone who has never attended church is much easier because they know they need a Savior. The ones who go once or twice a year believe they are already saved and don't need the Savior. It is a shame that the Shepherds do not teach their people to study the Bible for themselves. Through the Word is where genuine commitment begins.

It starts when the Angel pours out the seventh vial or bowl judgment, the last of the twenty-one plaques of Revelation, right before the second coming of Jesus and the battle of Armageddon.

16:17 "And the seventh angel poured out his vial into the air; and there came a great voice out of the temple of heaven, from the throne, saying, it is done."

16:18 "And there were voices, and thunders, and lightning; and there was a great earthquake, such as was not since men were upon the earth, so mighty an earthquake, and so great."

16:19 "And the great city was divided into three parts, and the cities of the nation's fell: and great Babylon came in remembrance before God, to give unto her the cup of the wine of the fierceness of his wrath."

16:20 "And every island fled away, and the mountains were not found."

16:21 "And there fell upon men a great hail out of heaven, every stone about the weight of a talent: and men blasphemed God because of the plague of the hail; for the plague thereof was exceeding great."

Notice that not only Babylon fell but also the cities of the nations (verse 19).

Also, don't forget the earth is already reeling from the thunder and lightning, not to mention the most significant earthquake the world has ever known.

Then, the great hail weighs about a talent (100 pounds each). This hail can destroy cities with no problem at all.

Then (verse 20) tells us that every island fled away, and the mountains were no longer found. It is the worst plague of the twenty-one by far as it destroys the political and commercial system called Babylon the Great from off the earth. Not to mention that this is the end of the planet as we know it, as it has been completely leveled and is ready for the coming renewal process.

CHAPTER 15
REVELATION 19

Revelation chapters 19 and 20 bring the climax of the Book of Revelation: the return of Christ to prove His Earthly Kingdom ("Kingdom – Christ's Coming Kingdom").

But first, the first five verses show heaven's response to the judgment of the harlot.

The multitude in heaven praises God for judging the great whore (Babylon, the harlot) and avenging the blood of the martyrs (7:9-17).

The eternal smoke symbolizes the permanence of Babylon's destruction (Isaiah 34:8-10). Amen derives from a Hebrew word meaning "to be firm" and may be translated as "truly" or "so be it."

This chapter is one of the most dramatic in the Bible. In it, the Church, the Bride of Christ, is the guest of honor at the marriage of the Lamb in heaven (verses 1-10) and returns with Christ in His Triumphal Second Coming (verses 11-21).

The people mentioned here are distinct from the other beings in heaven, for they are singing a song that includes mention of salvation. This scene incorporates believers, the Old Testament saints, the Church-age saints, and the Tribulation saints. Together, they join this great chorus proclaiming, "Alleluia!"

The scene now shifts from the earth, where it has been (since chapter 6), to heaven.

Verses 1-6: "Alleluia": This Hebrew word appears four times in the New Testament. This exclamation, meaning "Praise the Lord", occurs often in the Old Testament (Psalms 104:35; 105:45; 106:1;

111:1; 112:1; 113:1; 117:1; 135:1; 146:1).

Five reasons for their praise appear:

(1) God's deliverance of His people from their enemies (verse 1).

(2) God's meting out of justice (verse 2).

(3) God's permanent crushing of man's rebellion (verse 3).

(4) God's sovereignty (verse 6); and

(5) God's communion with His people (verse 7).

Revelation 19:1 "And after these things I heard a great voice of many people in heaven, saying, Alleluia; Salvation, and glory, and honor, and power, unto the Lord our God:"

In the last chapter, we saw the terrible destruction of commercial and political Babylon, symbolized by its capital city of Babylon. Now, the scene changes to heaven. We hear the voices of the redeemed. This "great voice" is because of the number of people speaking. It is not the size of each voice. These words of praise here are focused on the Lord Jesus Christ. The redeemed are the ones who are praised. There are not enough adjectives in the dictionary to say enough about what Jesus has bought for us all.

"After these things": This is a time key. After the destruction of Babylon at the end of the "Great Tribulation, just before the kingdom is proven (chapter 20). This section bridges the Tribulation and the millennial kingdom.

The marriage of the Lamb and the marriage supper of the Lamb "in heaven" (19:6-9) are evidence of the Church being in heaven before the return of Christ to earth.

Christ is the bridegroom at the marriage, and his Church is the bride. The word "church" (Greek ekklesia) appears nineteen times (in Revelation 1-3) and does not appear again until (Revelation 22:16), emphasizing the absence of the Church from the earth during the judgments of (Rev. chapters 4-18).

"I heard a great voice of many people in heaven": The people are the same as the 144,000 seen with the Lamb on Mount Zion (Revelation 14:1), and with those on the sea of glass, who had got the victory over the beast (Revelation 15:2), and are no other than God's covenant people, who are given to Christ, and made willing to be His in the day of His power.

And though they are a seed, a remnant, a small company, compared to the world and carnal professors, they are a large body of themselves.

Especially they will be now, when the nation of the Jews shall be born at once, and the fullness of the Gentiles will be brought in. Their voice on this occasion and the downfall of Rome is said to be "great" partly because of their number. Who will join in acclamations of praise, partly because of their extraordinary affection and intensity of spirit, which will be raised at this moment?

Revelation 19:2 "For true and righteous are his judgments: for he hath judged the great whore, which did corrupt the earth with her fornication, and hath avenged the blood of his servants at her hand."

"Judgments": Saints long for the day of judgment (6:10; 16:7; Isa. 9:7; Jer. 23:5). Godly people love righteousness and hate sin, for righteousness honors God, and sin mocks Him. Believers long for a world of justice, and it will come (verse 15; 2:27; 12:5).

It appears that those who were redeemed were looking on from heaven and approving of the destruction of Babel because the Messiah was bringing justice and righteousness to the world.

A reassuring tone here tells the Lord He was justified in His judgment. They have long waited for the time when God's justice would triumph. Now, that time had come.

"Which did corrupt the earth with her fornication": Drew the kings and inhabitants of the Roman empire into wicked and idolatrous practices, and so corrupted and destroyed them in soul, body, and

estate.

"And hath avenged the blood of his servants at her hand": And by these judicial dispensations God hath also taken vengeance on them for the blood of his saints shed by them. Remarkably, throughout this book, idolatry and persecution are made the beast's provoking sins.

Revelation 19:3: "And again they said, Alleluia. And her smoke rose forever and ever."

"Smoke rose": This is because of the fire (Rev. 17:16, 18; 18:8-9, 18; 14:8-11).

It says this judgment is permanent and is like God's language (Gen. 19:28). This statement tells us it will never be built again.

This destruction of the last, most powerful empire in history marks the end of man's day. The rebellion that had begun in the Garden of Eden has finally ended. Never again will there be more false religions, worldly philosophies, injustice, or unrighteousness. The entire sorry results of human depravity will finally be conquered.

Revelation 19:4: "And the four and twenty elders and the four beasts fell and worshipped God that sat on the throne, saying, Amen; Alleluia."

These twenty-four elders, I believe, as I said before, are two groups of twelve disciples and twelve Old Testament prophets. These are representatives of the church.

"Four beasts": The four beasts are the cherubim as described (in Rev. 4:6). These compose the same group as (in 7:11) and are associated with worship often (4:8, 11; 5:9-12, 14; 11:16-18).

Revelation 19:5: "And a voice came out of the throne, saying, praise our God, all ye his servants, and ye that fear him, both small and great."

The speaker isn't named but is probably an angel and refers to God as our one and only God. His instructions are to praise God.

The redeemed in heaven are called God's "Bond Servants," this is the group being addressed here to add to the other three mentioned groups.

"Both small and great": All distinctions and ranks must be transcended. The small and the great mean everyone, including all human categories and distinctions. All redeemed are told to praise God.

Verses 6-10: "*Omnipotent*": God is all-powerful and "reigns" over His universe. "*The marriage of the Lamb*": The *"wife" or bride of Christ* is the church (Matt. 22:2-14; John 3:29; 2 Cor. 11:2; Eph. 5:25-32), and the marriage is the eternal union of the church with Christ following the Rapture (1 Thess. 4:17).

The *"fine linen, clean and white"* stands for the "righteousness" of the church, which has now been judged and purified at the judgment seat of Christ (1 Cor. 3:12-15; 2 Cor. 5:10).

"The marriage supper of the Lamb" stands for the millennial kingdom of Christ, which will take place on earth following the return of Christ (20:4; Matt. 25:1-13; Luke 14:15-24).

"Called": Those invited to the marriage supper are Israel, who will turn to Christ in faith during the Tribulation (Jer. 31:31-34; Zech. 12:10; 13:9; Rom. 11:25-27). "Worship": Only God is to be worshiped (Rev.22:8- 9; Acts 10:25-26).

"Spirit of prophecy": The person and message of Jesus is the essence of all true prophecy.

Revelation 19:6: "And I heard as it were the voice of a great multitude, and as the voice of many waters, and as the voice of mighty thundering, saying, Alleluia: for the Lord God omnipotent reigns.

So vast is this group that they are without numbers. These are the faithful. When this great multitude begins to praise God, the volume would be so great as to sound like "mighty thundering."

"Lord God": Used many times in Revelation as a title for God (verse 15, 1:8; 4:8; 11:17; 15:3; 16:7, 14; 21:22). The great praise of

the multitude sounds like a massive crashing of waves.

This name used here, about our Lord, is very strange. It is the only place in the Bible where the word "*omnipotent*" occurs. Omnipotent means almighty: having unlimited power. When you couple that with "Lord," which means supreme in authority, and "God," which means supreme deity, you have an overwhelming understanding of Who this is.

Then we look at "*reigns.* It has no time element attached. It means continually reigns.

At this point, the evil world system has been destroyed, and God's kingdom has come into its fullness.

Revelation 19:7: "Let us be glad and rejoice and honor him: for the marriage of the Lamb has come, and his wife hath made herself ready."

The heavenly praise continues this time for a call for gladness, rejoicing, and giving God the glory for a fifth reason: the marriage of the Lamb has come.

"Marriage of the Lamb": Hebrew weddings consisted of 3 phrases:

(1) Betrothal (often when the couple were children).

(2) Presentation (the festivities that preceded the ceremony, often lasting several days).

(3) The ceremony (the exchanging of vows).

The church was betrothed to Christ by His sovereign choice in eternity past (Eph. 1:4; Heb. 13:20) and will be presented to Him at the Rapture (John 14:1-3; 1 Thess. 4:13-18). The final supper will signify the end of the ceremony.

This symbolic meal will take place at the establishment of the millennial kingdom and last throughout those 1000 years (21:2). While the term "bride" often refers to the church and does so here (2 Cor. 11:2; Eph. 5:22-24), it ultimately expands to include all the redeemed of all ages, which becomes plain in the rest of the book.

The marriage of the Lamb: The wife or bride of Christ is the church (Matt. 22:2-14; John 3:29; 2 Cor. 11:2; Eph. 5:25-32). And the marriage is the eternal union of the church with Christ following the Rapture (see 1 Thess. 4:17; see article "Rapture"). The fine linen, clean and white, represents the church's righteousness, which has now been judged and purified at the judgment seat of Christ (1 Cor. 3:12-15: 2 Cor. 5:10).

It is in total contrast to the harlot Babylon. Here, we see the chaste virgin (faithful to Jesus). At a marriage, there is rejoicing and giving of honor. The strange thing to me is that Jesus would even have us.

We have been washed in His blood and have our white wedding garments ready for the wedding. I believe the word "Lamb" is used here, instead of one of the other names of Jesus, to show that his sacrificial blood has cleansed us.

In ancient times, marriage was the most significant celebration and social event in the biblical world. Preparations and celebrations were much more elaborate than those of today. And they also lasted much longer.

They were in, *three distinct stages:*

1. Involving the wedding or engagement. It was an arrangement by both parents, was legally binding, and could only be broken by divorce. Then, there was a time of preparation as the groom prepared for his bride.

2. The presentation, a time of festivities just before the ceremony. Those festivities could last up to a week and sometimes even more, depending on the economic or social status of the bride and groom.

3. The wedding ceremony, during which time the vows were exchanged. The same imagery of a wedding pictures the Lord's relationship with His Church.

Revelation 19:8: "And to her was granted that she should be arrayed in fine linen, clean and white: for the fine linen is the righteousness of saints."

"Righteousness of saints": Not Christ's imputed righteousness granted to believers at salvation, but the practical results of that righteousness in believer's lives, i.e., the outward manifestation of inward virtue.

The *fine linen the bride* is clothed in stands for the righteous acts of the saints.

Just as I said, these robes have been made white by the blood of the Lamb. This "righteousness" was not ours until we received the Lord Jesus into our lives and took on His righteousness.

Our righteousness had been as filthy rags, but Jesus replaced the filth with His righteousness. Like many other places in the Bible, "her" does not mean just women; it is the bride. All believers in the Lord Jesus Christ are the bride of Christ, whether male or female.

I want to say a few words about this "fine linen." In the tabernacle in the wilderness, the High Priest wore a very ornamented robe with a breastplate of all sorts of jewels when he stood for God to the people, but when he went into the Holy of Holies, he wore pure white linen. You see, all the fineries of the world mean nothing to God. It tells us something about our approach to God.

Salvation is simple. It is not complicated; bear all to God. He knows all there is about us already. We do not have to pretend to be something we are not. He accepts us plain and simple.

Revelation 19:9: "And he saith unto me, Write, Blessed [are] they which are called unto the marriage supper of the Lamb. And he saith unto me, these are the true sayings of God."

"Blessed" (see note on 1:3).

"They which are called": This is not the bride (the church), but the guests. The bride doesn't get invited; she is asked. These are those saved before Pentecost, all the faithful believers saved by grace through faith up to the birth of the church (Acts 2:1).

Though they are not the bride, they still are glorified and reign with Christ in the millennial kingdom. It is differing imagery rather than differing reality. The guests will also include tribulation saints and believers alive in earthly bodies in the kingdom.

The church is the bride, pure and faithful, never a harlot, like Israel was (Hosea 2).

So, the church is the bride during the presentation feast in heaven, then comes to earth to celebrate the final meal (during the Millennium). After that event, the new order arrives, and the marriage is consummated (Rev. 21:1-2).

Those who are invited to the marriage supper are Israel ("*Marriage Supper*"), who will turn to Christ in faith during the Tribulation (Jeremiah 31:31-34; Zech. 12:10; 13:9; and Romans 11:25-27).

The marriage supper of the Lamb stands for the millennial kingdom of Christ, which will take place on earth following the return of Christ (20:4; Matt. 25:1-13; Luke 14:15-24).

The Jewish marriage consisted of three major elements:

(1) The marriage.

(2) The presentation.

(3) The marriage feast (supper), as was discussed just before.

Figuratively, about the church,

(1) The wedding takes place on earth during the church age.

(2) The presentation will take place in heaven following the Rapture (verse 7); and

(3) The marriage feast will occur on earth following Christ's return to the church.

Revelation 19:10: "And I fell at his feet to worship him. And he said unto me, see thou do it not: I am thy fellow servant, and of thy brethren that have the testimony of Jesus: worship God: for the testimony of Jesus is the spirit of prophecy."

"Fell at his feet": Overwhelmed by the grandeur of the vision, John collapsed in worship before the angel (1:17; 22:8).

"Do it not" (22:8-9). The Bible forbids the worship of angels (Col. 2:18-19).

John was so awed by all this that he fell at this angel's feet to worship him. Then, the angel quickly tells John not to worship him. Only God is to be worshiped (Acts 10:25-26).

"The testimony of Jesus is the spirit of prophecy": The central theme of both Old Testament prophecy and New Testament preaching is the gospel of the Lord Jesus Christ.

The *"testimony of Jesus"* is what the whole Bible is about. Without Jesus, there would be no salvation. The Old Testament points forward to Jesus, beginning in Genesis. The New Testament is the "last will" of Jesus; to receive our inheritance, we must read the will.

If you preach on prophecy, you are bringing the testimony of Jesus. If you understand the testimony of Jesus, then you must preach and prophesy so that others may live (The Bible"). This testimony here is not Jesus giving it, but we believers who testify of the Lord. Whoever this angel is, he, too, had the testimony of Jesus.

Verses 11-16: In these following six verses, we are swept up into the triumphal entourage of redeemed saints in the heavenly procession with the King of Kings. Jesus Christ comes to make war on Satan, the Antichrist, the False Prophet, and the kings of the earth.

He rides on a white horse and has on His head "many crowns." When this war with Satan is over, He becomes the absolute ruler of the earth.

Throughout the Old and New Testaments, the Scriptures teach Christ's literal, physical (bodily), and visible return to this earth to show His kingdom and rule for a thousand years. The most significant theme of all Bible prophecy is the second coming of Christ ("Glorious

Appearance – Second Coming of Christ").

It was the theme of humanity's first prophecy (Jude 14-15). Of the last messages of the Bible (22:20). While certain events and experiences may occur in the lives of individuals (Christ appearing to those who are saved or to those who die), these are, of course, not the ultimate return of Christ.

The Second Coming should be reserved for His final revelation at the end of the age. In anticipation of the Second Coming, Christians should live soberly, righteously, and godly (Titus 2:12; see Jude 14, Rom. 2:1-16, besides the scriptures here in 11-16).

This *"white horse"* is not that of 6:2. Here, the *"True" Messiah* returns in victorious conquest. He is *"Faithful"* to His Word and promises. He will fulfill the twofold role of *"judge" and warrior.* His judgment of the earth will be righteous (Rev.16:5-7; 19:2; Psalm 96:13).

The *"fire"* depicts glory and judgment. The "crowns" show total sovereignty and authority (12:3; 13:1).

The secret *"name"* expresses the mystery and greatness of the person of Christ (Rev. 2:17; 3:12; 19:13, 16; Phil. 2:9-11).

The *"blood" stands for the judgment* of Christ's enemies (Rev. 14:14-20; Isa. 63:1-6).

The name "*Word of God*" presents Christ as the revelation of God Himself (John 1:1, 14, 1 John 1:1). In His first advent, Jesus especially revealed the love and grace of God (John 1:17; Rom. 5:8).

But in His second advent, He will reveal the holiness, justice, and judgment of God (compare Heb. 4:12).

Revelation 19:11: "And I saw heaven opened, and behold a white horse, and he that sat upon him was called Faithful and True, and in righteousness, he doth judge and make war."

"Heaven opened": The One who ascended to heaven (Acts 1:9-11) and had been seated at the Father's right hand (Heb. 8:1; 10:12;

1 Peter 3:22) will return to take back the earth from the usurper and show His kingdom (5:1-10). The nature of this event shows how it differs from the Rapture.

At the Rapture, Christ meets His own in the air; in this event, He comes with them to earth. At the Rapture, there is no judgment; in this event, it is all judgment. This event is preceded by blackness, the darkened sun, the moon gone out, stars fallen, smoke, then lightning, and blinding glory as Jesus comes. Such details are not included in Rapture passages (John 14:1-3; 1 Thess. 4:13-18).

"White horse": In the Roman triumphal processions, the victorious general rode his white war horse up the Via Sacra to the temple of Jupiter on the Capitoline Hill. Jesus' first coming was in humiliation on a colt (Zech. 9:9).

John's vision portrays Him as the conqueror on His war horse, coming to destroy the wicked, overthrow the Antichrist, defeat Satan, and take control of the earth (2 Cor. 2:14).

Notice several things about the description of our Lord's return.

1. It will be public, clear, and not restricted to a small group. He says His coming will be like lightning, those flashes from the east to the west. Everybody will see it, and there will be no hiding it.

2. He says it will occur "immediately after" the Great Tribulation.

3. His return will be accompanied by "mourning" by "all the tribes of the earth."

The mourning of sadness on the part of the Jewish nation, that it so long rejected Christ as Messiah, as well as the mourning of despair on the part of the ungodly, who reject Him as King even as He appears in the sky.

This opening of heaven is not to go in but is the opening for Jesus and His followers to come out.

Again, as we saw in chapter four, a door opened in heaven; the door to heaven has never been closed for the Christians to enter.

The *"horse" symbolizes war,* and the fact that it is "white" stands for victory.

White also symbolizes holiness and righteousness. It tells us that this war is holy, and Jesus is victorious.

"Faithful and True": True to His word, Jesus will return to earth (Matt. 24:27-31; see note on 3:14).

The fact that "Faithful and True" has initial caps lets us know that this figure is God the Son, who has been made Lord of lords and King of kings, and Jesus is the Judge. He is always faithful to His promises, and what He says is always true.

"In righteousness, he doth judge" (20:11-15; Matt. 25:31; John 5:25- 30; Acts. 17:31). We are assured that His judgments are right. He has been sitting at the Father's Right Hand in heaven, but now He is about to set up His kingdom here on the earth.

"Wages war": This startling statement, appearing only here (and 2:16), vividly portrays the holy wrath of God against sinners (Psalm 7:11). God's patience will be exhausted with sinful, rebellious humanity.

The most detailed description of the ("Second Coming"), was given by our Lord Himself in Matthew:

Matthew 24:27: "For as the lightning comes from the east and flashes to the west, so also will the coming of the Son of Man be."

Matthew 24:29-31 "Immediately after the tribulation of those days the sun will be darkened, and the moon will not give its light; the stars will fall from heaven, and the powers of the heavens will be shaken." "Then the sign of the Son of Man will appear in heaven, and then all the tribes of the earth will mourn, and they will see the Son of Man coming on the clouds of heaven with power and great glory." "And He will send His angels with a great sound of a trumpet, and they will gather His elect from the four winds, from one end of heaven to the other."

Revelation 19:12: "His eyes were as a flame of fire, and on his head were many crowns, and he had a name written, that no man knew, but he."

"His eyes were as a flame of fire": "Eyes" show wisdom, and these, like "flames of fire," can see right into the soul of man. Nothing escapes His penetrating vision, so His judgments are always just and accurate (see note on 1:14).

This *"fire"* here speaks of purity and judgment. The crowns show total sovereignty and authority (12:3; 13:1). The secret name expresses the mystery and greatness of the person of Christ (2:17; 3:12; 19:13, and 16; Phil. 2:9-11).

"A name no man knew": John could see the name but could not understand it (2 Cor. 12:4). There are unfathomable mysteries in the Godhead that even glorified saints cannot grasp.

A secret name was on the stone underneath the High Priest's breastplate worn into the Holy of Holies. It was the unspeakable name of God. This name here is like that name.

It is a name that no one knew except our Lord. In (Rev. 3:12), we studied about this name the Lord will put on us.

Revelation 19:13: "And he was clothed with a vesture dipped in blood: and his name is called The Word of God."

"A vesture dipped in blood": This is not from the battle of Armageddon, which will not have begun until verse 15. Christ's bloodspattered garments symbolize the great battles He has already fought against sin, Satan, and death and has been stained with the blood of His enemies.

It does not stand for Jesus's blood on the cross but is a picture of judgment, not redemption. However, it is the blood of his slaughtered enemies. It is not His first battle but his last. He has fought for His people throughout redemptive history, and his "war clothes" bear those stains. The blood stands for the judgment of Christ's enemies

(14:14-20; Isaiah 63:1-6).

"The Word": Only John uses this title for the Lord (the introduction: Author and Date). As the Word of God, Jesus is the image of the invisible God (Col. 1:15), the express image of His person (Heb. 1:3), and the final, complete revelation from God (Heb. 1:1-2).

Over and over in these lessons, I have given the Scriptures where the word of God took on the form of flesh and dwelt among us. In the first chapter of the book of John, we read about the Word of God.

John 1:1: "In the beginning was the Word, and the Word was with God, and the Word was God."

Jump down to.

John 1:14: "And the Word was made flesh and dwelt among us, (and we beheld his glory, the glory as of the only begotten of the Father,) full of grace and truth."

We also see here that this Word (Jesus) was, is, and always will be God the Word.

Verses 14-16: Christ is King over all who call themselves kings, and Lord over all who call themselves lords (17:14; Deut. 10:17; Dan. 2:47; 1 Tim. 6:15). Here we see the Second Coming of Christ as the armies in heaven come with Him.

Revelation 19:14: "And the armies which were in heaven followed him upon white horses, clothed in fine linen, white and clean."

"Armies ... in heaven": Composed of the church (verse 8), tribulation saints (7:13), Old Testament believers (Jude 14; Dan. 12:1-2), and even angels (Matt. 25:31). They return not to help Jesus in the battle (they are unarmed), but to reign with Him after He defeats His enemies (20:4; 1 Cor. 6:2; 2 Tim. 2:12; Psalm 149:5-9).

They will share in Christ's victory and glory (Romans 8:18-19).

The linen symbolizes righteousness (verse 8).

Here, we see the believers in the Lord Jesus Christ following: the called, chosen, redeemed, and bride. The whole army is on "white horses." They have white horses because they have overcome the devil. They are washed in the blood of the Lamb. They have on pure white linen for the righteousness of Christ. This army has been in heaven waiting for the wrath of God on the ungodly to be over.

Revelation 19:15: "And out of his mouth get a sharp sword that with it he should smite the nations: and he shall rule them with a rod of iron: and he trod the winepress of the fierceness and wrath of Almighty God."

"Sharp Sword": This symbolizes Christ's power to kill His enemies (1:16; Isa. 11:4; Heb. 4:12-13). That the sword comes out of His mouth shows that He wins the battle with the power of His word. Though the saints return with Christ to reign and rule, they are not the executioners. That is His task.

The sword from His mouth depicts judgment through His spoken Word (1:16; 2:12-16; Isaiah 11:4; 2 Thess. 2:8). The Bible says that it is so sharp that it can divide the soul and spirit.

Hebrews 4:12: "For the word of God is quick, and powerful, and sharper than any two-edged sword, piercing even to the dividing asunder of soul and spirit, and of the joints and marrow, and is a discerner of the thoughts and intents of the heart."

Smite the nations: Christ will destroy all unbelievers (19:21; Matt. 25:41-46; 2 Thess. 1:8-9). Rod of iron: Christ will subject all nations to Himself and destroy all His enemies (Psalms 2:8-9; 1 Cor. 15:24-25). Winepress (14:17-20).

"Rod of iron: Swift, righteous judgment will mark Christ's rule in the kingdom. Believers will share His authority (2:26; 1 Cor. 6:2; see note on 2:27; 12:5; Psalm 2:9).

Words relating to wrath and anger are found 15 times in Revelation. We see how powerful this Word is. This "rod of iron" that He is to rule with means that His law is absolute and unwavering. He never changes.

"Winepress": A vivid symbol of judgment (14:19; Isa. 63:3; Joel 3:13).

When we see this, "tread the winepress of the fierceness and wrath," " this wrath of God is for three and a half years of Tribulation, then after those, another three and a half years that is called the Great Tribulation, making a total of seven years of God's Judgment and Wrath.

Revelation 19:16: "And he hath on [his] vesture and his thigh a name written, KING OF KINGS, AND LORD OF LORDS."

"On His thigh": Jesus will wear a banner across His robe and down His thigh with an emblazoned title emphasizing His sovereignty over all human rulers (Rev. 17:14).

"KING OF KINGS, AND LORD OF LORDS": Christ has universal sovereignty. It expresses His sovereign triumph over all foes and absolute rule in His soon-to-be-set-up Kingdom. (17:14; Deut. 10:17; Dan. 2:47; 1 Tim. 6:15).

There are approximately ninety-seven names throughout the Bible that the personage we know as Jesus is used.

The name He was called at the time had to do with the circumstance at hand. Here, He is coming to the earth to take over as Supreme Ruler, so He is called "KING OF KINGS AND LORD OF LORDS."

Verses 17-21: These verses depict the frightening holocaust unparalleled in human history, the Battle of Armageddon, the pinnacle of the Day of the Lord (1 Thess. 5:2). It is not so much a battle as execution as the remaining rebels are killed by the Lord Jesus (verse 21; 14:19-20; Psalm 2:1-9; Isa. 66:15-16; Ezek. 39:1; Joel 3:12; Matt. 24:25; 2 Thess. 1:7-9).

This Day of the Lord was seen by Isaiah (66:15-16), Joel (1:15; 3:12- 21), Ezekiel (39:1-4; 17-20), Paul (2 Thess. 1:6; 2:8), and our

Lord (Matt. 25:31-46).

Verses 17-18: "The supper of the great God" differs from the marriage supper of the Lamb (verse 9). Here, God calls the "fowls" or birds of the sky to "gather" to "eat the flesh" of those who have died in the Battle of Armageddon 16:14, 16; 19:21; Ezek. 39:17-20).

"All men" shows "all kinds of men"; not everyone at Armageddon will be an unbeliever (Matt. 25:31-46).

Revelation 19:17: "And I saw an angel standing in the sun; and he cried with a loud voice, saying to all the fowls that fly amid heaven, Come and gather yourselves together unto the supper of the great God;"

An angel speaking in a loud voice invites all the birds to feed on the results of the carnage that will shortly take place.

This angel is declaring Christ's victory before the battle even begins. A similar passage (Luke 17:37) states that the eagles (vultures) will gather wherever the corpse is.

"The supper of the great God": Also called "the war of the great day of God, the Almighty" (16:14). It will begin with an angel summoning birds to feed on the corpses of those who will be slain (Matt. 24:27-28). God will declare His victory before the battle even begins. The Old Testament often pictures the indignity of carrion birds feasting on human dead (Deut. 28:26; Psalm 79:2; Isa. 18:6; Jer. 7:33; 16:4; 19:7; 34:20; Ezek. 29:5).

This "supper" that this speaks of will be right after the battle of Armageddon. Some people believe the birds are gathering in Israel now for the feast ("Armageddon").

"Unto the supper of the great God": As if the great God were about to give you a feast, to wit, the carcasses of those slain. It is called "His supper" because He gives it; the image is that there would be a great slaughter of His foes, as specified in the following verse.

Revelation 19:18: "That ye may eat the flesh of kings, and the flesh of captains, and the flesh of mighty men, and the flesh of horses, and of them that sit on them, and the flesh of all men, both free and bond, both small and great."

What this is saying is that for those lying out there dead in the valley of Megiddo, it will not matter whether you were a general or a private. The birds will not know the difference. With God, there has never been a distinction. He is not impressed with your position in life. The birds will eat them all.

It reveals the extent of the massive slaughter. To have one's unburied body left as food for birds would be the ultimate indignity, especially for the mighty military commanders and the proud kings.

The same fate awaits the God-hating rebels everywhere in the world.

Verses 19-21: The "armies" of the "beast" and the "kings" of the East (and of all the "earth") will gather in Palestine at Armageddon (16:12- 16) to try to prevent the return and kingdom of Christ. Christ will defeat and capture the Beast and the "false prophet" (Rev. 13).

These will become the first inhabitants of the "Lake of fire" (Rev. 20:10). The rest of the kings and armies will be killed by the Word of Christ and will be eaten by the birds (verses 17 and 18). The unbelieving survivors of the Tribulation will be judged by Christ and sentenced to everlasting fire (Matt. 25:41, 46).

Revelation 19:19: "And I saw the beast, and the kings of the earth, and their armies, gathered together to make war against him that sat on the horse, and against his army."

"Kings of the earth" (17:12-17).

"Their armies": (16:13-14).

"His army": Zechariah describes this army of the Lord as "all the holy ones" (Zech. 14:5).

This beast is the Antichrist, the leader of human history's last and greatest empire. The kings of the earth are those ten kings who rule the ten sectors into which the Antichrist's worldwide empire is divided.

The Antichrist has gathered his armies to battle Jesus and His army. With all its firepower, the formidable and seemingly invincible armed might of the beast now awaits the arrival of the Rider on the white horse.

Ever since the beginning of time, the armies of God and the armies of the devil have been in mortal combat. The flesh and the Spirit have been in battle also. Isaac (Spirit) and Ishmael (flesh) are still in mortal physical combat through their descendants in Israel today.

The Scripture above speaks again of the battle of Armageddon.

Revelation 19:20: "And the beast was taken, and with him the false prophet that wrought miracles before him, with which he deceived them that had received the mark of the beast, and them that worshipped his image. These both were cast alive into a lake of fire burning with brimstone."

"The beast was taken ... the false prophet": In an instant, the world's armies are without their leaders. The beast is the Antichrist (13:1-8); the false prophet is his religious cohort (13:11-17).

"Cast alive": The bodies of the beast and the false prophet will be transformed, and they will be banished directly to the lake of fire (Dan. 7:11), the first of countless millions of unregenerate men (20:15) and fallen angels (compare Matt. 25:41), to arrive in that dreadful place.

These two still appear there 1000- years later (20:10), refuting the false doctrine of annihilationism (14:11; Isa. 66:24; Matt. 25:41; Mark 9:48; Luke 3:17; 2 Thess. 1:9).

But before the battle can even begin, it's over. Not only that but those two demonically empowered leaders, Antichrist and False Prophet, are dealt a terrible blow. Those two are thrown alive into the lake of fire.

Satan used the false prophet and the beast to perform his evil deeds. As the two most evil, vile, and profane people who have ever lived, it is fitting that they should be the first two to arrive in that awful place.

And they will be there by themselves for a thousand years until the devil joins them at the end of the millennium.

Then, at the second resurrection (the second death), they will be joined by all unbelievers for all eternity.

"Lake of fire": The final hell, the place of eternal punishment for all unrepentant rebels, angelic or human (20:10, 15). The New Testament says much of eternal punishment (14:10-11; Matt. 13:40-42; 25:41; Mark 9:43-48; Luke 3:17; 12:47-48).

It is the first mention of the "lake of fire" in the Bible. It is the final hell and the ultimate destination of Satan, his angels (or demons), and the unredeemed ("Hell, for the Unbelieving Dead").

Hell has always existed, but this is hell's final form. Unlike Hades, which was a temporary holding place, this was the last permanent place for incarceration and punishment.

"Lake of fire burning with brimstone" (9:17. These two are often associated with divine judgment (14:10; 20:10; 21:8; Gen. 19:24; Psalm 11:6; Isa. 30:33; Ezek. 38:22; Luke 17:29).

We see the total victory over the beast and the false prophet here. It shows here that the *"KING OF KINGS"* throws them into the "lake of fire." This "brimstone" is sulfur. It is the final victory over the earthly manifestations of Satan's power.

Revelation 19:21: "And the remnant was slain with the sword of him that sat upon the horse, which [sword] proceeded out of his mouth: and all the fowls were filled with their flesh."

Then, all the rest who were with the Antichrist and the false prophet will be destroyed, and the rest of those gathered to fight against Christ.

"Sword" (15; Zech. 14:1-13).

Then, suddenly, it will be all over. There will not be any war at all as we think of fighting. The Rider sitting on the white horse will speak just a word. That's the same One who spoke the heavens and the earth into existence at the very beginning. The One who said to a fig tree, and it withered away.

Who spoke to the howling winds and heaving waves. The storm clouds vanished, and the waves were stilled. Who said to a legion of demons in a man, and instantly, they fled.

Now, by His Word, *the Beast is stricken where he stands.* The false prophet windbag from the pit is stilled. Then they're hurled into the everlasting flames. Then another Word and all the panic-stricken army stagger and fall dead.

"Fowls were filled with their flesh": All remaining sinners in the world will have been executed, and the birds will gorge themselves on their corpses. All the birds ate and were filled with the flesh of those killed.

The rest of the unredeemed throughout the world will be judged at the sheep and goat judgment, which takes place at this time (Matthew 25:32-46; "*Judgment on Mankind is Coming*").

It is not just defeat but physical death for those who followed the beast and the false prophet. The Word of God overthrew them.

They die in the battle of Armageddon by the Words of Christ and not by an easy death, as scripture tells us that the blood in that valley ran up to the horse's reins, about 4 to 5 feet deep for the entire length of the 200- mile valley.

CHAPTER 16
THE SEVEN PRINCES OF HELL

Mythology & History

Y ou will have likely heard of the seven deadly sins, a famed classification of vices or behavioral traits commonly perceived as the most negative. But did you know that according to some scholars, these seven sins are each personified by a particular demon, a prince of Hell, to be more precise? So, who were these lords of sin, and what did they stand for? Let's find out together. (Raconteur - Mythology & History, 2023).

Narrator: "Satan is the most powerful demon…"

The Four Crown Princes of Hell:

- Lucifer,

- Satan,

- Leviathan, and

- Belial.

Eight Dukes of Hell:

- Astaroth,

- Asmodi,

- Oriens,

- Ariton,

- Magoth,

- Beelzebub,

- Paymon, and

- Amaymon.

Seven Deadly Sins

- Escanor: *Lion's Sin of Pride.* (Lucifer)

- Merlin: *Boar's Sin of Gluttony.* (Beelzebub)

- Gowther: *Goat's Sin of Lust.* (Asmodeus)

- King: *Grizzly's Sin of Sloth.* (Belphegor)

- Ban: *Fox's Sin of Greed.* (Mammon)

- Diane: *Serpent's Sin of Envy.* (Leviathan)

- Meliodas: *Dragon's Sin of Wrath.* (Satan)

Four corners of the earth:

- North

- South

- East

- West.

Seven Sin- Seven Demon Prince

- Pride - Lucifer

- Wealth - Mammon

- Lust - Asmodeus

- Envy - Leviathan

- Gluttony - Beelzebub

- Wrath - Satan

- Sloth – Belphegor

SEVEN PRINCES OF HELL

You will have heard of the seven deadly sins, a famed classification of vices or behavioral traits commonly perceived as the most negative.

But did you know that according to scholars, these seven sins are each demon, a prince of Hell, to be more precise?

So, who were these lords of sin, and what did they stand for?

While many different classifications of demons exist across the centuries, one of the most well-known is The Seven Princes of Hell, written by Peter Binsfeld, a German bishop. He was a well-respected man of his time, considered particularly intelligent, and associated heavily with witchhunting. His writings about witches and demonology remain the most influential today.

His most famous work, however, was his 1589 classification of the seven princes of Hell. He assigned one demon to each of the seven deadly sins in his text.

This list has become the most widely referenced classification of the seven princes and their associated representations.

- *The first demon is Lucifer, who stands for one of the most despised sins - pride.*

LUCIFER - DEMON OF PRIDE

Though the name and its meaning of "morning star" or "light bringer" have a variety of applications in many religions, it is used here to refer to the angel who fell from Heaven after he tried to overthrow God and create a new structure of power, thus showing the evil of pride.

Therefore, he is the leader of the demons in Hell and is particularly dangerous. Early medieval thinking commonly distinguished Lucifer and Satan as two separate entities, as we will soon see in the case of the classification of the seven princes.

While Lucifer, as the devil, is in Hell, Satan executes the desires of Lucifer as his vassal. More recently, however, Lucifer and Satan are considered interchangeable.

- The second demon prince is Mammon, who stands for the sin of greed.

MAMMON - DEMON OF GREED

Another fallen angel, Mammon, was greedy even while in Heaven, and it was suggested that part of his fall was because he openly valued Heaven's gold streets above his feelings for God. However, more recent translations of the Bible tend to translate the word "Mammon" as literal, Greed or wealth; Binsfeld and others of his time viewed him as a demonic figure who lured humans to evil deeds through the promise of great wealth.

- The Third prince of Hell is Asmodeus, the demon of lust

ASMODEUS - DEMON OF LUST

Often depicted with three heads, one of a bull, one of a human, and one of a ram, as well as a variety of other animal-like parts, the book of Tobit claims Asmodeus killed the seven husbands of Sarah on the night of her wedding, just before they were able to consummate the marriage, to prevent her marrying anyone else.

He is also quoted in the book of Solomon as claiming that he "Is always hatching plots against newlyweds; I mar the beauty of virgins and cause their hearts to grow cold."

Named by Pope Gregory the Great as one of the fallen angels, Asmodeus was the punisher of crimes of lust in the classification of Binsfeld.

- *Fourth in the list is the Demon of Envy, the mighty Leviathan.*

LEVIATHAN - DEMON OF ENVY

In many religions, the Leviathan is known as a gigantic sea monster. Still, it seems unlikely Bins shared this view, who claims Leviathan is a prince of Hell responsible for punishing the envious.

St. Thomas Aquinas was one of the earliest to propose Leviathan as the punisher of envious sinners, but why is unclear.

In the writing of Father Sebastien Michaelis, which is based on the testimony of a demon, Leviathan was said to handle tempting people toward sacrilege, which, at the time, referred to literal theft rather than a general sense of thwarting the will of the church and God.

It is plausible that assigning Leviathan as the overseer of envy comes from him encouraging people to steal from the church.

- *The fifth demon is Beelzebub, the prince of gluttony*

BEELZEBUB - DEMON OF GLUTTON

Sometimes, Beelzebub is painted as a fallen angel and a high-ranking demon in Hell. Often interchangeable with Lucifer or Satan, other sources name him as the chief lieutenant to Lucifer and suggest he played a role in the demon revolt against Satan.

Beelzebub is known by many names, including "Lord of the Flies" and "Baal."

The reference to flies and flying could be connected to his ability to fly and his links to disease.

According to other scholars, he was the demon being proud or envious, but Binsfeld associated Beelzebub with gluttony.

- The sixth demon is Satan himself, the Lord of wrath.

SATAN - DEMON OF WRATH

As mentioned earlier, Satan is often interchangeable with other demons such as Beelzebub or, most commonly, Lucifer.

But in classifying the seven princes of Hell, he is a distinct demon standing for the sin of wrath. Because Satan is often conflated with Lucifer, some overlap in their histories – Satan is also said to be an angel who fell from Heaven for rebelling against God.

'Satan' is translated to 'the adversary,' in this case the adversary of humanity. Whereas God is loving and wise, Satan is wrathful towards society. Often seen as Hell's ruler, Satan is one of - if not the - most powerful demon.

- *The Seven demon prince is Belphegor, the Lord of Sloth.*

BELPHEGOR - DEMON OF SLOTH

It is perhaps unsurprising that this demon was chosen to stand for sloth, given his image is one of the least intimidating of the Seven Princes of Hell, as he's often depicted just sitting on a toilet.

However, there is more to his story, as this prince of Hell is also associated with trickery and deceit.

He seduces and manipulates humans into creating ingenious inventions that will make them rich by revealing secrets and making suggestions that lead to amazing discoveries with the promise of great wealth.

But when these are complete, Belphegor snatches the wealth and esteem away.

It is suggested that this promise of great wealth is connected to no longer having to work, encouraging the sin of sloth or laziness.

According to famed demonologist and witch hunter Peter Binsfeld, that completes the seven princes of Hell. Each demon personifies one of the seven deadly sins.

These figures have appeared in different religious texts in various forms across the years, often standing for other ideas and associated with differing threats of punishments. Still, this classification keeps a popular place in modern thinking. I suppose only one question is still.

Which of these princes of Hell with their seven vices might you see soon?

The term hell is cognate to *"hole" (cavern)* and *"hollow"*. It is a substantive formed from the Anglo-Saxon *"to hide".* This verb has the same primitive as the Latin and the Greek. Thus, by origin of hell denotes a *dark and hidden place.* In ancient Norse mythology, *Hel is the ill-favored goddess of the underworld.* Only those who fall in battle can *enter Valhalla;* the rest go down to *Hel in the underworld,* not all, however, to the place of punishment of criminals.

CHAPTER 17
WHERE IS HELL?

S ome believed that hell is everywhere, that the damned are at liberty to roam about in the entire universe, but that they carry their punishment with them. The believers of this doctrine were called Ubiquity, or Ubiquitarians; among them were, e.g., _Johann Brenz, a Swabian, a Protestant theologian of the sixteenth century._

However, that opinion is universally and deservedly rejected; for it is more in keeping with their state of punishment that the damned be limited in their movements and confined to a certain place. Moreover, if hell is a real fire, it can be everywhere, especially after the consummation of the world, when heaven and earth shall have been made anew.

As to its vicinity, all kinds of speculations have been made; it has been suggested that hell is situated on some far island of the sea, or at the two poles of the earth; Swinden, an Englishman of the eighteenth century, imagined it was in the sun; some assigned it to the moon, others to Mars; others placed it beyond the confines of the universe (Wiest, VI (1789), 869).

The Bible seems to indicate that hell is within the earth, for it describes hell as an abyss to which the wicked descend. We even read of the earth's opening and the wicked sinking into hell (Numbers 16:31, Psalm 54:16; Isaiah 5:14; Ezekiel 26:20; Philippians 2:10,).

Is this merely a metaphor to illustrate the state of separation from God? Although God is omnipresent, He is said to dwell in heaven, because the light and grandeur of the stars and the firmament are the brightest manifestations of His infinite splendor. But the damned are utterly estranged from God; hence their abode is said to be as remote as possible from his dwelling, far from heaven above and its light, and consequently hidden away in the dark abysses of the earth. However, no clear reason has been advanced for accepting a symbolic interpretation in preference to the most natural meaning of the words of Scripture.

Therefore, theologians generally accept the opinion that hell is really within the earth. The Church has decided nothing on this subject; therefore, we may say hell is a certain place; but where it is, we do not know.

St. Chrysostom reminds us: *"We must not ask where hell is, but how we are to escape it". Saint Augustine says: "It is my opinion that the nature of hellfire and the location of hell are known to no man unless the Holy Ghost made it known to him by a special revelation"*, (City of God XX.16).

Elsewhere he expresses the opinion that hell is under the earth. St. Gregory the Great wrote: *"I do not dare to decide this question.* Some thought hell is somewhere on earth; others believe it is under the earth"; (1763).

Existence of hell

There is a hell, i.e. all those who die in personal mortal sin, as enemies of God, and unworthy of eternal life, will be severely punished by God after death. On the nature of mortal sin, - SIN; on the immediate beginning of punishment after death, Particular Judgment. As to the fate of those who die free from personal mortal sin, but in original sin, Limbo.

The existence of hell is, of course, denied by all those who deny the existence of God or the immortality of the soul. Thus, among *the Jews the Sadducees, the Gnostics, the Seleucidan, and in our time Materialists, Pantheists, etc.,* deny the existence of hell. But apart from these, if we abstract from the eternity of the pains of hell, the doctrine has never met any disagreement worthy of mention.

The existence of hell is proved first from the Bible. Wherever Christ and the Apostles speak of hell they take for granted the knowledge of its existence (Matthew 5:29; 8:12; 10:28; 13:42; 25:41, 46; 2 Thessalonians 1:8; Revelation 21:8).

It is a very complete development of the Scriptural argument, especially regarding the Old Testament, which may be found in (Christlike Eschatology 1890).

Also, the fathers, from the very earliest times, are undisputed in teaching that the wicked will be punished after death. And in proof of their doctrine, they appeal both to Scripture and to reason.

The Church acknowledges her faith in the Athanasian Creed: "They that have done good shall go into life everlasting, and they that have done evil into everlasting fire."

The Church has repeatedly defined this truth, e.g. in the profession of faith made in the Second Council of Lyons in 464 and the Decree of Union in the Council of Florence in 693: *"the souls of those who depart in mortal sin, or only in original sin, go down immediately into hell, to be visited, however, with unequal punishments.*

If we abstract from the eternity of its punishment, the existence of hell can be established even by the light of simple reason. In His sanctity and justice as well as in His wisdom, God must avenge the violation of the moral order in such wise as to preserve, at least in general, some proportion between the seriousness of sin and the sternness of punishment.

But it is evident from experience that God does not always do this on earth; therefore, He will inflict punishment after death. Moreover, if all men were fully convinced that the sinner needed fear no kind of punishment after death, moral and social order would be seriously jeopardized.

However, Divine wisdom cannot permit it. Again, if there were no reckoning beyond that which takes place before our eyes here on earth, we should have to consider God very unsympathetic to good and evil, and we could in no way account for His justice and holiness. Nor can it be said: the wicked will be punished, but not by any positive infliction: for either death will be the end of their existence, or, surrendering the rich reward of the good, they will enjoy some lesser degree of happiness.

These are chances and vain maneuvers, unsupported by any sound reason; positive punishment is the natural reward of evil. Besides, the due proportion between fault and punishment would be reduced impossible by an indiscriminate eradication of all the wicked. And finally, if men knew that their sins would not be followed by sufferings, the mere threat of eradication now of death, and still less the prospect of a somewhat lower degree of beatitude, would not do to deter them from sin.

Furthermore, reason easily understands that in the next life, the just will be made happy as a reward for their virtue (Heaven). But the punishment of evil is the natural counterpart of the reward of virtue.

Therefore, there will also be punishment for sin in the next life. Accordingly, we find among all nations the belief that evildoers will be punished after death. This universal conviction of mankind is additional proof aimed at the existence of hell. For it is impossible that, regarding the ultimate questions of their being and their destiny, all men should fall into the same error; else the power of human reason would be scarce, and the order of this world would be unduly wrapped in mystery; this, however, is offensive both to nature and to the wisdom of the Creator.

On the belief of all nations in the existence of hell. (2nd ed., Münster, 1869, 1878). The few men who, despite the morally universal conviction of humanity, deny the existence of hell, are mostly atheists and Epicureans.

But if the view of such men in the fundamental question of our being could be the true one, apostasy would be the way to light, truth, and wisdom.

Eternity of hell

Many admit the existence of hell but deny the eternity of its punishment. Conditionalizes hold only proposed immortality of the soul and declare that after undergoing a certain amount of punishment, the souls of the wicked will be annihilated.

Among the Gnostics the Valentinians held this doctrine, and later also Arnobius, the Socinians, and many Protestants both in the past and in our times, especially of late (Edw. White, "Life in Christ", New York, 1877).

The Universalists teach that in the end all the damned, at least all human souls, will attain beatitude. This was a tenet of the Origenists and the Misericords of whom St. Augustine speaks. There were individuals advocates of this opinion in every century, e.g. Scotus Eriugena; in particular, many rationalistic Protestants of the last centuries defended this belief, e.g. in England, Farrar, _"Eternal Hope"_ (five sermons preached in Westminster Abbey, London, and New York, 1878).

Among Catholics, Hirscher and Schell have recently expressed the opinion that those who do not die in the state of grace can still be converted after death if they are not too wicked and impenitent.

The Holy Bible is quite clear in teaching the eternity of the pains of hell. The torments of the damned shall last forever and ever (Revelation 14:11; 19:3; 20:10). They are everlasting just as are the joys of heaven (Matthew 25:46).

Of Judas Christ says: _"It were better for him, if that man had not been born"_ (Matthew 26:24). But this would not have been true if Judas was ever to be released from hell and admitted to eternal happiness.

Again, God says of the damned: _"Their worm shall not die, and their fire shall not be quenched"_ (Isaiah 66:24; Mark 9:43, 45, 47). The fire of hell is repeatedly called eternal and unquenchable. The wrath of God abides on the damned (John 3:36); they are vessels of Divine wrath (Romans 9:22); they shall not possess the Kingdom of God (1 Corinthians 6:10; Galatians 5:21).

The objections presented by Scripture against this doctrine are so meaningless that they are not worth discussing in detail. The teaching of the fathers is not less clear. We merely call to mind the testimony of the martyrs who often declared that they were glad to suffer the pain of a brief duration to escape eternal torments.

Origen indeed fell into error on this point; but precisely for this error, he was condemned by the Church (Canons III, 279, 211).

However, Unsuccessful attempts were made to undermine the authority of these canons (Münster, 1899, 137). Besides even in Origen we find the orthodox teaching on the eternity of the pains of hell; for in his words, the faithful Christian was again and again victorious over the doubting philosopher.

Then Gregory of Nyssa seems to have favored the errors of Origen; many, however, believe that his statements can be shown to be in harmony with Catholic doctrine.

But the suspicions that have been cast on some passages of Gregory of Nazianzus and Jerome are decided without justification. The Church professes her faith in the eternity of the pains of hell in clear terms in the Athanasian Creed in trustworthy doctrinal decisions (In 211, 410, 429, 807, 835, 915), and in countless passages of her church service; she never prays for the damned. Hence, beyond the possibility of doubt, the Church expressly teaches the eternity of the pains of hell as a truth of faith that no one can deny or call to question without clear sacrilege.

HELL

The Latin Infernus (infirm,), the Greek Hades, and the Hebrew sheol correspond to the word hell. Infernus is derived from the root in; hence it designates hell as a place within and below the earth. Haides, formed from the root, to see, and a privative signifies an invisible, hidden, and dark place; thus is the term hell. The origin of sheol is doubtful. It is generally supposed to come from the Hebrew root meaning, *"to be sunk in, to be hollow"*; accordingly, it signifies a cave or a place under the earth.

In the Old Testament (Septuagint hades; Vulgate Infernus) sheol is used quite in general to label the kingdom of the dead, of the good (Genesis 37:35) as well as of the bad (Numbers 16:30); it means hell in the strict sense of the term, as well as the limbo of the Fathers.

But, as the limbo of the Fathers ended at the time of Christ's Ascension, hades (Vulgate Infernus) in the New Testament always designates the hell of the damned. Since Christ's Ascension they just no longer go down to the lower world, but they dwell in heaven (2 Corinthians 5:1). However, in the New Testament, the term Gehenna is used more frequently in favorite to hades, as a name for the place of punishment of the damned.

Gehenna is the Hebrew Gehinnom (Nehemiah 11:30), or the longer form gê-ben-Hinnom (Joshua 15:8), and gê-benê-Hinnom (2 Kings 23:10) *"valley of the sons of Hinnom".* Hinnom seems to be the name of a person not otherwise known. The Valley of Hinnom is south of Jerusalem and is now called Wadi er-rababs. It was tarnished as the scene, in earlier days, of the horrible worship of Moloch.

For this reason, it was defiled by Josias (2 Kings 23:10), cursed by Jeremias (Jeremiah 7:31-33), and held in abomination by the Jews, who, accordingly, used the name of this valley to designate the abode of the damned. And Christ adopted this usage of the term. Besides Hades and Gehenna, we find in the New Testament many other names for the abode of the damned.

The different places of Hell is called:

- *"Lower Hell"* (Tartarus) (2 Peter 2:4),

- *"Abyss"* (Luke 8:31),

- *"Place of Torments"* (Luke 16:28),

- *"Pool of Fire"* (Revelation 19:20 and),

- *"Furnace of Fire"* (Matthew 13:42, 50),

- *"Unquenchable Fire"* (Matthew 3:12,),

- *"Everlasting Fire"* (Matthew 18:8; 25:41; Jude 7),

- *"Exterior Darkness"* (Matthew 7:12; 22:13; 25:30),

- *"Mist" or "Storm of Darkness"* (2 Peter 2:17; Jude 13).

The state of the damned is called:

"Destruction" (Philippians 3:19),

"Perdition" (1 Timothy 6:9),

"Eternal Destruction" (, 2 Thessalonians 1:9),

"Corruption" (Galatians 6:8),

"Death" (Romans 6:21),

"Second Death" (Revelation 2:11).

Hell (inferno) in theological tradition is a place of punishment after death.

Theologians distinguish four meanings of the term hell:

- *Hell* in the strict sense, or the place of punishment for the damned, be they demons or men.

- *The Limbo of infants (limbus parvulorum),* where those who die in original sin alone, and without personal mortal sin, are confined and undergo some kind of punishment.

- *The Limbo of the Fathers (limbus partum),* in which the souls of the just who died before Christ awaited their admission to heaven; for in the meantime heaven was closed against them in punishment for the sin of Adam.

- Purgatory, where the just, who die in pardonable sin or who still owe a debt of chronological punishment for sin, are cleansed by suffering before their admission to heaven.

REFERENCES:

Raconteur 2023- Mythology & History

Holy Bible 2012, Spiritual Warfare Bible, Charisma House Book Group. 600 Rinehart Road, Lake Mary, Florida 32746

The Lost Books of the Bible, Nicodemus, Pg.82-88,1926.